Culture 101

Creating places where people thrive
and profits grow

Penny Nesbitt

First published by Busybird Publishing 2017
Copyright © 2017 Penny Nesbitt
Re-released 2026

ISBN
Print: 978-1-925585-94-0
Ebook: 978-1-925585-63-6

Cover image: Kev Howlett, Busybird Publishing

Cover design: Busybird Publishing

Layout and typesetting: Busybird Publishing

Editor: Anna Bilbrough

Busybird Publishing
2/118 Para Road
Montmorency, Victoria
Australia 3094
www.busybird.com.au

Contents

What People Are Saying ...

Workplace culture, leadership, productivity and Positive Psychology: for me, these go hand-in-hand. Penny has put these things together in a simple, easy to read and practical way. I have lived my life and set up my business around the practical application of these areas and I know that books that provide real, tangible and practical tools are infrequent. Penny's language is real and all her own and her engaging style is worth the time spent. Enjoy!

Sue Langley, CEO - *The Langley Group*

Penny doesn't just talk about culture — she builds it, lives it and challenges others to take ownership of it. Culture 101 is a practical, no-nonsense guide that cuts through the noise and gets to the heart of what actually drives high-performing teams. In my work across complex organisations, I see firsthand how difficult it is to move from intention to action when it comes to culture. Penny bridges that gap with clarity, honesty, and real-world application. This book is not just a read — it's a toolkit for leaders who are serious about creating environments where people and performance thrive.

Nadia Pessarossi, Director - *Pulse8 Strategies*

The difference between theory and application is experience. Knowing the theory of swimming does not mean you will survive when thrown into the water. Penny Nesbitt is a swimmer. Been there, done that. She brings decades of deep wisdom to the art and science of building a working culture that actually works!

Colin James - *The Colin James Method*

Penny's ability to adapt her style of facilitation to a range of different audiences ensures that both the privilege and responsibility of leadership remain top of mind for all of us, as does the need for ongoing reflection and learning in order to achieve personal and business goals.

Steve Tillett, *Head of Human Resources*

Penny worked hand-in-hand with me on the design and delivery of an in-house leadership development program, offering suggestions and posing questions throughout to make sure the specified business requirements were met, and always tailoring her delivery style to the target audience. The roll-out of the program across Australia over a two-year period led to significant and positive middle-management culture change in a major agribusiness.

Nina Langley, *Director of Human Resources*

Penny has a finely tuned sense about the way people think and behave, offering practical and innovative ways to bring out their best. Whether working with leaders, functional teams or front-line employees, Penny facilitates conversations and learning sessions that help drive businesses forward.

Sharon Cartwright, *Strategic Communication Consultant*

No surprise that Penny was writing a book, even less surprising was her subject matter. Penny lives and breathes this stuff! Collaborating with Penny on leadership development over a number of years demonstrated not only her own strengths and positivity, but also her desire to build engagement through workplace dialogue. Her ability to really engage through conversation and particularly in a training room creates wellbeing at work for those around her. She has an engaging style that, combined with her smarts and wit, can't help but exude happiness!

Vicki Thompson, Learning and Development Consultant - *WrestPoint Casino*

Penny's skills and insights have been incredibly valuable as I set up a new business. First, when hiring – educating and guiding me to work out what skills and personal characteristics we needed – and, later, in building an effective team. Her methods brought quick results!

Linda Tizard, Managing Director - *The Broad Picture*

About this Book

If:

- You are deliriously happy at work most days, and can't wait to get in there

- You love your job, in fact, you can't believe they actually pay you to work there

- You have a fantastic boss who you trust implicitly – and that's a two-way thing

- You feel your career's on track, you're stretched and challenged but never set up to fail

- You're part of a team that's able to talk openly about and come to agreement on difficult, sometimes ambiguous, contentious stuff with no 'blood on the floor'; no feelings being hurt; no 'meetings after the meeting'; no fear of ridicule or recriminations for holding a 'left of field' perspective; no politicking, gossiping or back-stabbing

- You're pretty much allowed to be, and applauded for being, yourself, and supported in doing what you're best at rather than just trying to do your best

- You all adhere to high levels of accountability and ownership so that GANT chart you're all working to moves along smooth as

… Firstly, where do you work? A few other readers may be very interested …

Secondly, this might not be the book for you. Unless though, you're not quite sure what the recipe is for building and sustaining this kind of thriving and productive culture, and would maybe like some easy-to-implement ideas.

Boss, manager, or team member, there's a big difference between fluking a great culture and knowing what it takes to create, sustain and drive it. Or to start turning things around if your culture, let's not mince words here folks, basically sucks.

If the wealth of information from engagement and climate surveys is anything to go by, we have something of a problem on our hands when it comes to company culture. A **70 BILLION Australian dollars per year** problem, according to a 2016 Gallup report on the cost of disengagement. That is a staggering amount of money by any standard, especially in a country of just over 23 million people. And if, like many companies, you have a lot of Millennials working for you, they now make up the largest percentage of the workforce, and the largest percentage of the disengaged.

And we're not alone. According to the Gallup report, we're one of the luckier countries when it comes to employee engagement. Worldwide cumulatively only 13% of people say they're actively engaged at work. That starts to ring some serious alarm bells when you line up those sorts of numbers against company results for things like safety, customer satisfaction, profitability, turnover and innovation.

Think about it. When was the last time you regularly leapt out of bed, eager to get to work? Or had a really good belly laugh with the team? What ground-breaking, catalytic, career-defining epiphany did you gain from your last performance review?

Each day, when you step into that workspace, for most of the day are you able to be the same you that walked out of your front door? Are you firing on all cylinders most of the time or do you feel kind of like a Ferrari that someone bought to drive to the local shops in? And how often are you and your team doing what you know you're really, really great at and love doing?

Running employee development programs over a couple of decades, my own experience is a microcosm of that sobering Gallup research. And it's what's inspired me to put pen to paper (fingers to laptop, actually).

In workshop after workshop, particularly when I'm running leadership programs for future or existing leaders, after a day or two of enthusiastic and engaged participation, all too often the question gets asked that goes something like this: '… This is great stuff, makes so much sense … Learning a lot … How come my leader doesn't do this/isn't doing this program … Why isn't our company doing this?'

To be honest, I'm usually stumped for an answer to that question. That's in situations where senior leaders (those who in essence drive the overall culture) have approved the development program, but don't seem to think it's necessary for them to attend a 'higher-ups' version of what's being rolled out, clarifying the part they play in walking the talk, thereby getting the best ROI (Return On Investment) on the program, and making sure any changes have the best chance of sticking. Bizarre really. Especially when you go back and look at those eye-watering figures on what disengagement and toxic cultures are costing.

Occasionally people share stories, either in the group or privately later, about a leader's behaviour that frankly falls into the category of 'truth is stranger than fiction' – some of these stories are seriously the stuff of a Hollywood writer's dreams.

(And it's just this sort of work culture that no doubt explains why it's estimated we take this sort of stuff from work to home, at six times the rate that home troubles come the other way.)

Another disturbing fact: more heart attacks and sudden deaths amongst working people happen on a Monday than on any other day of the week, driven apparently by a massive surge of the stress hormones adrenaline and cortisol. Toxic cultures are basically killing people.

So, inspired by these stories and by my own mind-numbing, soul-destroying experiences of toxic cultures, a couple of bosses from hell and a confidence-draining redundancy or two, I decided it was time to do my bit in terms of making a difference.

As I've been doing research for *Culture 101*, and studying Positive Psychology at the same time, it's been a powerful affirmation that I've been on the right track – for quite some time actually. Even in those dark days as I wandered, slightly bewildered and a tiny bit more deflated from corporate job to corporate job, until I took matters into my own hands and began working for myself. As one client put it on hearing about *Culture 101*, 'Pen, this is great, it's what you've been banging on about for years'.

Silver bullets I don't have. I can, however, share some insights, stories, easy-to-implement tools, great resources, plus some pearls of wisdom from people who are leading lights in all things culture; people from larger companies getting it right through to everyday people in small businesses who seem to have something pretty special going on when it comes to culture.

Interview with Sue Langley, CEO, The Langley Group

(This interview has been lightly edited for clarity and readability.)

In March 2017, I was thrilled to be able to interview Sue Langley, CEO of The Langley Group.

Sue is an international expert on the practical applications of Positive Psychology, neuroscience and emotional intelligence and travels constantly around the globe, spending most days doing what she loves and is great at – key-note speaking, conference presentations and facilitating development or accreditation programs.

Sue was in Auckland when I interviewed her after being on her feet all day, yet still made time to talk to me. If you're ever lucky enough to meet Sue, she is the living embodiment of what *Culture 101* is all about – tireless, exudes positive energy, generous with her time and walks the talk in terms of what she's passionate about.

Penny Nesbitt: Hi Sue, thanks again for your time. As I mentioned, the book I'm writing is called *Culture 101: Creating places where people thrive and profits grow.* Sue, when you think about culture and its impact on people's thriving and company profitability, what sorts of things come to mind?

Sue Langley: I think culture is absolutely essential; it's intangible, yet it influences everything. If you think about the culture of the organisation, it is defined as 'what happens around here' and the way that people behave so it can have a huge impact. Is it a culture of openness and trust and honesty and respect and collaboration and all those sorts of things, or is there a fear of failure culture, is there a lack of trust across the team and things like that? I suppose when I think of culture, I also think of it in terms of climate. What's the climate like for people within the organisation? I think it's essential to many things, particularly people thriving. If you think of an individual, if I'm not supported and engaged in my workplace, my wellbeing is impacted, and the profitability of the company is impacted.

Penny Nesbitt: What about positive leadership and the leader's impact on culture?

Sue Langley: Thinking about positive leadership, it depends a bit on which framework you look at. I use Kim Cameron's model. Positive leadership is basically about creating a positive climate, one where positive emotions predominate over negative. It's about creating a culture of meaning, where people feel that they're engaged in work that contributes to something bigger or more important than their individual tasks and aligns to their values. It's about positive relationships, where people are striving and connected and leveraging their strengths every day. And it's about positive communication, where again there is more supportive and affirmative language as opposed to the negative or constricting language. And if I think about the impact of that, it is essentially to ourselves, because we're no longer in a situation where people command and control work or people, not that they ever really did. People want more from work than just being employees; they want more opportunities. So, therefore, from a leadership perspective, if we're not really connecting to the heart of who somebody is and we're driving people just through tasks, well it's not going to work.

Penny Nesbitt: What about when difficult things happen? When I talk about Positive Psychology, a lot of people seem to have a bit of a mistaken view of what it's all about, and one of the things that I'm at pains to point out is that it's not just about focusing on positive things, it's important also to take lessons from things that aren't working. People often say, 'Well what about when bad things happen? What about organisations that are struggling?' They've had to make redundancies, for example. How does Positive Psychology become relevant then?

Sue Langley: I think it's even more relevant then, because it's easy when things are going well, when you don't have to worry about things quite so much. To me, positive leadership becomes even more important when we're dealing with those challenges, because you can do redundancies in a supportive and engaging way, or you can do it in a less effective, distrustful way. If I take a real-life example of somebody who came off one of our programs at the end of last year … I actually saw him recently and he stood up and shared an example of how he views what he learnt to the exec team.

He said that he had to do a restructure where he had to make people redundant and give people feedback and with everything he learnt about positive leadership, positive coaching, etc., he said he was really surprised that every single one of those conversations went well. He was expecting some really challenging conversations with some real difficulties, but because he could put into practise what he learnt, he was surprised and pleased that those conversations were positive.

I think this is even more important when things aren't going so well; that you can tap into people's strengths and help them get through it, and you can really bond together with the positive relationship side of things so that people do see that they're being supported and they're being collaborated with and still being communicated with in an open and positive way. So, it's actually more essential when things are not going well. When things are going well, nobody thinks about the sense of meaning, because you've just got it anyway. When you're having a bad day that meaning and sense of contribution becomes even more important to be clear about.

Penny Nesbitt: And what about the people left behind? There's very few people these days that have escaped their career without being made redundant, once, twice, sometimes more and often what happens is that the people that are left behind have other people's work tasks thrust on them, if you like. What happens then in terms of people being able to operate to their strengths? What's the danger?

Sue Langley: Well, there are dangers, except I always believe that if you've got a positive climate then it makes it easier. If you've got a challenging climate in the first place, then it's going to make it harder.

So assuming that you have a positive climate and you engender the climate of trust and support and positive emotions and all those sorts of things, then yes, of course you've got the social rejection that happens when people are made redundant and you've also got the people left behind, feeling, potentially, survivor guilt, having more work to do and things like that, so of course there's those things there. I guess for me again this is where Positive Psychology comes in, in that if we've actually taught people strategies about how to build their positive emotions, how to build their resilience, how to look after themselves in this way, then when adversity hits you're more able to deal with it. We know from all the research that it's how you are when things are going well that will also help serve you when adversity comes along. So for me, again it's important we teach people before the adversity hits, so that we've got those things in practise. It becomes really important to you when applied when adversity occurs.

Penny Nesbitt: So, what are some key questions that you think leaders should be asking themselves in their teams, if they are genuinely interested in starting to turn around a culture that is clearly not thriving?

Sue Langley: Look, I think there's honesty here and a certain question you should ask yourself is how I show up. A question that I love is, 'Do I energise a room more when I enter it or when I leave it?' And I think that is such a powerful question as a leader to be asking yourself. What sort of culture or climate have I created? What impact am I having? We know from the [Hay Group] research that the leader's emotional state contributes to about 70% of the climate of the team, so basically the first question should be, how am I showing up? Am I showing up as the best version of myself more frequently, because you can't expect a high-performing, positive culture to create itself if you're volatile yourself, if you're expressing negative emotions more frequently than positive emotions, if you're not actually trusting people. The other question I'd be wanting to ask is, 'Am I playing to my strengths as a leader?' Because all the research tells us that if I as a leader am developing myself to my strengths, then I'm actually perceived as a more effective leader.

Penny Nesbitt: One of the mistakes that people make, I'm sure you would agree, is people thinking they have to turn themselves inside out and become someone else.

Sue Langley: Absolutely.

Penny Nesbitt: A question that came up recently was around authentic leadership and I'm interested to hear your thoughts on that, because people often think that's being purely yourself, warts and all, 100% of the time, which isn't my understanding of what authentic leadership's about, so what's your thoughts on that, Sue?

Sue Langley: Look, my area of expertise is the positive relationship side of things and to me authentic leadership and positive leadership go hand-in-hand. It's again how am I showing up, not that I can be myself warts and all and just throw it all out there and who cares, it is about showing up as the best version of me. How do I show up more frequently as the best version of me? Yes, I'll have bad days, yet have I got the authenticity to acknowledge that, to be aware of my emotions and apologise when I've stuffed up, as opposed to not facing up to it, dealing with it – which to me is not authentic leadership.

Penny Nesbitt: Sue, look, thanks very much. So many great insights there.

Sue Langley: Of course, you are more than welcome.

Chapter 1

DANGER! HAZMAT AREA!

The beatings will continue until morale improves.
Attributed to Captain Bligh
Mutiny on the Bounty

Culture – what exactly is this thing called culture? What makes it? What 'breaks' it? And how, if things aren't exactly thriving, do you start to breathe life back in to your flailing culture?

Ask anyone what culture is and you get a lot of admirable yet somewhat vague, typically can't nail it to the wall answers. '…We're really into teams ... No silos here ... We provide massages, karaoke, fruit ... People are our most valuable assets ... We believe in autonomy'. (Seriously? Has anyone ever admitted to being a world-class micro-manager who breathes down your neck and never delegates?)

Perhaps you've already tried to turn things around culture wise – strategised, analysed, theorised, downsized, rightsized, agonised and prophesised. Maybe you've called in the consultants, gone through a bit of a change initiative, perhaps even been lucky enough to have done an awesome refurb or moved offices to a fabulous new state-of-the-art fit out.

And yet, at best, things are still definitely not what you'd call 'humming' around here.

At its worst, according to your latest 'climate' survey, employee engagement is at an all time low. At the same time, turnover's at an alarming high, mental health days have become standard fare, and it's clear there's a lot of 'presenteeism' going on – people turning up to work but leaving hearts, initiative and discretionary effort at home. Productivity is dipping rapidly and you can't seem to get any new ideas off the ground.

(I once had a young person in the new team I was managing say to me, ' … You know, the culture around here is so toxic that they should issue Hazmat suits at the front door!' Cripes – *just stop right there* and think about the implications of that statement. You wear a Hazmat suit to protect your health and wellbeing, to stop you from being infected or affected by something that is VERY dangerous and hazardous to your health. And this is the mindset people had as they were turning up to work every day? Not exactly conducive to all those marvellous things that contribute to people and companies thriving.)

Maybe, just maybe then, it's time to take a long hard look at your culture. You know, that sort of 'amorphous mass' that everyone knows about, yet can't quite put a defining finger on. That thing that prospective new employees want to know all about so that they can work out if your company is right for them – or not.

According to reams of research, it's your culture – how people feel about working at your company – that will determine whether you hang on and just survive (or worse), or thrive, along with all those amazing people you've employed.

It's the difference between that sinking, sleep-depriving, keeps-you-awake-at-night feeling, knowing that you're constantly in catch-up mode, constantly replacing those high-demand, hard-to-find people that you just can't seem to hang on to. Constantly ten steps behind your biggest competitor, constantly worrying about that major client who, let's face it, brings in most of your income and is being wooed by your competitor – the place to where all these ex-employees are defecting. It's the difference between that and building, innovating and thriving, and yes, having a bit of fun while you're doing it.

Fact is, and you might not want to hear this, ultimately, people are not coming to work to help you achieve your dreams. Drill that into your brain – no, they're not, sorry to disappoint you.

They're there to achieve their own dreams. Whatever those dreams may be – a holiday, new home, kid's education, a new car, a new pair of shoes.

BUT – and there is a BUT – they will *must definitely* give their all, including their discretionary effort, the incredible ideas generated in their amazingly innovative brains, their hearts and minds – in return for you treating them as the awesome individuals that they are. You know, those innate qualities, traits and personal strengths – the things you saw on their resume and then behaviourally interviewed the hell out of them during the recruitment process. The things that they love doing, are good at and that totally switch on their lights.

Keys to Thriving

They'll do all this when some things line up that will make your culture hum, your company become sought after, your productivity and profitability climb, customers happier, turnover drop and your sleepless nights become a thing of the past. Things critical to your culture thriving that go across everything else that are seemingly simple, yet take perseverance, dedication and commitment to instill and to maintain. But, I promise that the rewards, personal, financial and otherwise are well worth it.

What are these things?

First things first: people want to rock up to work in a place that has a sense of meaning and purpose connected to what they value, working for bosses that they trust. And, given that we spend most of our waking hours at work, people want to be able to use their natural strengths, the things they love doing, want to do more of and that really light them up. I'm going to be talking a lot about strengths. What that means at work, how to spot them, and why they matter waaaaaay more than weaknesses.

And unless Will Smith and his android buddies from *I, Robot* have taken over your company, I'm assuming you still employ actual flesh and blood human beings. So, we'll take a good look at the links between a positive thriving culture and many aspects of wellbeing, why fostering wellbeing is crucial, and the link between this and your profitability. I'll also be talking about a bit more than the free annual flu shot, the basket of week-old fruit in the kitchen or the dusty gym equipment in the basement.

In yet another Gallup research study[1] (good old Gallup, where would I be without their wealth of information?) they sum up what I've been talking about for years, often unfortunately falling on deaf ears.

The Millennials study captured what it seems most of us want at work, what Gallup calls The Big Six when it comes to work culture. What are The Big Six? Not some uber cool updated version of The Magnificent Seven, but six critical, sound, positive, people-focused changes to foster in your culture.

____

1 - *How Millennials Want to Work and Live*, Gallup Inc., 2016

THE BIG SIX is about the shift from:

My Pay Cheque	to	My Purpose
My Satisfaction	to	My Development
My Boss	to	My Coach
My Annual Review	to	My Ongoing Conversation
My Weaknesses	to	My Strengths
My Job	to	My Life

This also sums up beautifully what *Culture 101* is all about, drawing on scientifically researched, evidence-based information about what sort of conditions lead to people being able to flourish, to thrive, to be at their best – ultimately a win/win for employee and employer.I'll also be talking a lot about our ancestors, those folks who evolved to survive the harshness of the Savannah, kept it together, were incredibly creative and outwitted a conga line of predators, all basically leading to you being able to sit here today, reading this book.

Now while that might possibly sound strange, living as most of us do in large, humming, complex, sophisticated, technologically advanced societies, our bodies haven't changed much since then. Maybe a bit less hair, we're definitely taller, our life expectancy is generally longer and our brains have got bigger.

But, the things that really drive us, things that generally happen with little or no conscious awareness, those systems that evolved all that time ago, systems designed to keep us together for survival, they're still pretty much unchanged. And that, as you'll come to see, is very relevant if you want your people to thrive, be at their best and so contribute to a highly profitable company.

Be yourself, everyone else is taken
Oscar Wilde

People who know me well know that I've always prided myself on being a little bit 'different'. Not break-the-law, different for different's sake, whacky, waaaaaay left of field, stuff-the-establishment kind of different.

Just someone who gets a kick out of (and is pretty good at actually!) finding novel solutions to problems, challenging conventional thinking when people are stuck, and dressing a little outside the bog-standard 'black suit, stockings and high heels' uniform.

(Some years ago, my then manager told me that our MD had described my style as a bit bohemian – I was, clearly, ahead of the fashion curve! I was wearing the obligatory uniform of black skirt suit, stockings and heels, with a beautifully tailored top that featured an asymmetrical hem. I smiled when she told me, and taking it as compliment – remember, this was said to someone who loves the idea of being a little bit left of field – I said with a big smile on my dial, 'Really?'. Her frosty response? 'It was *not* a compliment!')

So, it never ceases to baffle me when I hear some companies talking about the success of their diversity policy. Absolutely necessary, was a long time coming, and has certainly made huge positive improvements in opportunities for many people.

But, for some companies this diversity policy seems to stop short when it comes to people who dare to be a bit different, to be themselves, who want to be able to use their strengths at work, so they're fulfilled and happy, with the (profoundly and unarguably scientifically researched) side effect that the company thrives as well.

Seems to me though, and the myriads of people I talk to, plus no doubt those who show up as actively disengaged in survey after survey, that very soon after people join a company the pressure to comply, to be like everyone else, begins. You've just employed this awesome human being with all this knowledge, individual gifts, strengths, traits, intuition, initiative and now let's just knock that all out of you and get on with all of us being the same.

The thing is, you see, people are human, people are 'messy', people have stuff going on at home and sometimes they don't do things exactly the way you thought they were going to do them. That's essentially what makes us all so amazing, unique and innovative!

When Bad Things Happen to (Your) Good People

Perhaps, like me, you've been made redundant a couple of times. REDUNDANT. What's that a euphemism for exactly? I think we all know: surplus to requirements, we don't need/ want you, your services/skills are no longer required, you're fired, you don't fit, you're not valued …

I do a lot of work with people who've fallen foul of the latest round of redundancies and, even though it's commonplace now, people in the main still report a range of distressing self-confidence diminishing thoughts, feelings and emotions when it happens. Even if they've been fed that old chestnut, 'It's not personal, it's just a business decision'.

Give me a break! You just gave me the flick and it's not personal?

For many people, this is a sick-making moment, as your now former employer takes control of your life and things spin out of control. And here's a sobering fact I learned recently that goes a long way to explaining the psychological, emotional and physical impact of redundancy, particularly if there's been any kind of slow freezing-out process going on as the unsuspecting 'redundee' approaches the fatal day: the neural pathway for social rejection is the same neural pathway as that for traumatic physical pain. Just let that sink in for a moment; havwe a think about the psychosical safety implications. And now think about it in the context of rolling redundancies, business silos, teams that don't get on, dismissing, ostracising or rejecting someone because they're different, and, of course, bullying.

This is one of those ancient, survival-of-the-species mechanisms, as being and remaining part of the 'herd' ensured survival back in the early days of humankind So, feeling a level of pain equivalent to being physically attacked is a sure fire way of diminishing behaviour that could threaten your own or the group's survival. Great system for survival!

Yet not so great if you start to sense something is going on, you notice you're not getting as many of those group emails or meeting invitations, and a couple of people seem to be avoiding you altogether.

Going back to the redundancy scenario, maybe the reality is that the company has skidded so far down the not-thriving slope that some tough decisions have had to be made. People who you'd rather not lose, well, you just can't afford them anymore.

Fact is, as science now tells us, if you get the culture right, if you get people lined up doing what they love doing and are good at, look after them and have them connected to a real sense of purpose and meaning, you won't be doing so much in the way of redundancies or losing people you really need.

Also, take a moment to think about those poor souls left behind who've somehow managed to survive rolling restructures and redundancies. The standard resolution for what to do with BAU[2] and WIP's[3] is that those left standing just take over the dearly departeds' jobs, along with their own work. And so the cultural erosion continues unfettered, as people hunker down, relieved at some level that they at least have a job, yet miserable, disengaged, focused on surviving rather than thriving, and just trying to do their best, rather than what they're best at, in the hope that they're not next.

During the depths of the 1990s recessionary period, when unemployment was at an all-time high, along with soaring interest rates, I was 'lucky enough' to have a job. Day after day, I recall crying on my way to work (now there's a clue!) because I hated the job so much but was too scared to speak up about my bullying boss for fear of losing my job. So, like many others, I hunkered down and basically ticked off the requirements of the job description.

Seems I wasn't alone in my pre-work lacrimation, as it appears from chats with numerous people working in toxic cultures that distress or the tears on the way to work thing is sadly not uncommon. How your people are feeling about going into work on a Sunday evening is also a pretty accurate litmus test of where your culture is headed.

Under psychological threat, our brains pretty much go into Paleo mode – not the diet, but the operating mode necessary for survival of the species, the fight or flight response, triggered by two mighty little units called the amygdalae on either side of the brain. They act like sort of a bouncer, deciding what events or information they'll let through to the hallowed halls of the pre-frontal cortex, and what things won't, things that herald a threat to your survival.

Effectively then, when we perceive a threat, as deemed by the amygdalae, a whole physiological process is initiated

---

2 - Business As Usual
3 - Work In Progress

that's aimed at either gearing up for a fight for survival, or getting out of there as fast as possible. And, when the perceived threats are psychological, the amygdalae become overly sensitised to anything that could indicate a threat. Performance management anyone? Can I give you some feedback? Office invite with the boss and HR at 10am, Monday?

Ever had a situation where the stakes were high (e.g. job or no job), where it's often a case of she said/he said, opinions clearly differ and the emotional temperature rises quickly? Ever noticed how, a few hours afterwards, you come up with some real pearlers, thinking to yourself, 'Why didn't I say that?' In situations like these, I've heard myself say, 'It was like my brain went to mush', which, it turns out, is a fairly apt description!

When it's a significant threat, such as that 10am meeting with HR, your amygdalae are highly likely to go into full-blown flight or fight mode, shutting down access to your working memory and triggering the release of a cascade of hormones like adrenalin and cortisol to do their job of preparing your body for fight or flight.

Along with pumping up muscle, raising your heart rate so more oxygen can get to those muscles and a whole lot more, part of the process leads to the temporary shutdown of access to the calm, rational, creative, innovative part of our brains and our working memory. Back in the day, when it was a case of eat or be eaten, this was not the time for pontificating about whether you're fit enough to fight, or if your dicky knee's healed enough to outrun the would-be diner. So, let's just get that pesky and (potentially fatal) pontificating part of the brain out of the way while we gear up for survival.

Thinking back to that dreaded 10am meeting … Not fair really, when you think about it, as it's now virtually impossible for you to hold your end of a rational discussion, and you will be that way for about three hours until your body and your brain can return to normal operating level. I'll cover more about this in the chapter where I look at feedback, when, for most people, the good old amygdala bouncer has got 'Can I give you some feedback?' right at the top of the 'no-fly' list.

The bottom line is that even when things are becoming increasingly uncertain, when people feel generally insecure, unsafe or under threat, the amygdalae become vigilant. Maybe not fully, 'You're not getting in' kind of bouncer mode, but enough that people 'bunker down'; continuing to do what they've always done – what's the norm or safe – developing a bit of a 'siege' mentality and closing off from being creative. Pretty much 'survival' techniques aimed at reducing stress, ambiguity and fear, and generally geared at making sure they keep their jobs.

As Maslow might very well have pointed out, it's pretty hard to be contributing to 'corporate self-actualisation' when your employees are getting a clear message that their means of survival, of putting a roof over their heads and food on the table, appears to be very much under threat.

Ultimately, what you'll get is a drastic reduction in the return on your investment in these awesome people, and hence the inability to reap the rewards of one of the very things that make us human – the ability to think creatively.

Diverse ... to a Point

So, how much and what kind of diversity or individuality does your company 'tolerate'? In the December 2007 issue of FastCompany [4], Ryan Matthews and Watts Wacker (terrific name for a bloke talking about being different!) outline their thoughts on innovation. Deviance or individuality, they say, 'is the source of all innovation. It's the wellspring

---

4 - FastCompany December 2007, *Deviants Inc.* Ryan Matthews & Watts Wacker

of ideas, new products, new personalities, and, ultimately, new markets ... nothing more or less than any one of us taking one measurable step away from the middle of the road'.

And what do they say gets in the way of more companies taking that first tentative step?

' ... In one company after another, corporate culture serves as an organisational prophylactic, protecting business-as-usual businesses from new opportunities. In truth, many corporate cultures work to eliminate deviant employees. Corporate culture works to discourage deviant ideas. Corporate culture punishes deviant behavior and attitudes. And, of course, as a result, most large companies lose the opportunity to discover the future and get there first.'

I hear a lot of people talking about the need to be far more creative and innovative and, given how often the topic comes up, there seems to be a bit of a conflict at play here. For every company struggling to come up with new, catalytic, leading-edge ideas, you can bet that there's something of an internal cultural dilemma around the appetite for difference, diversity of ideas, or deviance from the hallowed norms of whatever industry you're in, and the drive to make sure everyone toes the line, the drive for conformity and BAU.

Fundamentally, what science now tells us, is that to have a creative edge you need to grow and sustain a culture that's based on positive leadership; where people are doing what they're best at most of the time, wellbeing is a priority and they're in a workplace where they can see that what they do connects to a strong, company-wide, lived and embraced sense of meaning and purpose.

KEY TAKEAWAYS

- How people feel about working at your company, the culture, will determine whether you hang on and just survive (or worse) or thrive.

- People aren't coming to work to help you achieve your dreams; they're coming to work to achieve their own dreams.

- People want to rock up to work in a place that has a sense of meaning and purpose connected to what they value, what's important for them.

- People want to be able to use their natural strengths, the things they love doing, want to do more of and that really light them up.

- The neural pathway for social rejection is the same neural pathway as that for physical pain.

- When things are becoming increasingly uncertain, when people feel generally insecure, unsafe or under threat, the amygdalae become vigilant.

- To have a creative edge you need to grow and sustain a culture that tolerates wide-ranging diversity, that's based on positive leadership, where people are doing what they're best at most of the time, and in a workplace where they can see that what they do connects to a strong sense of meaning and purpose.

REFLECTION QUESTIONS

- On a scale of one to ten, one being catching people doing something wrong most of the time, ten being catching them doing something right most of the time, where would you put your company?

- How do you feel about your job right now?

- What are your strengths? (Hint: these are typically things you love doing, do a lot of or would like to do more of and that really energise you.)

- Where's your company on The Big Six right now?

Chapter 2

NOSE DIVING OR THRIVING?

What lies behind us and what lies before us are
tiny matters compared to what lies within us.

Ralph Waldo Emerson

Some time ago, I had the great good fortune to go to the 'Zoo with a View', Sydney's Taronga Park Zoo, where the animals have enviable views across Sydney's stunning harbour. As we walked about, listening to the various keepers and zoo guides, I was taken by the incredible amount of detailed research, time, thought and care put in to creating habitats for the various animals.

Fundamentally, the habitats are designed to be as close as possible to the animal's 'real world', to ensure that the animals aren't stressed, are healthy, are able to get all the nutrients they need from food, sleep well and relax, are able to operate at their best, and, as the zoo is involved in global breeding programs for many species, to give them the best chance of surviving.

Then I got to thinking about what humans would need if we were to have a habitat designed for us to be at our best. Not just bricks and mortar, but how people feel about working there. Yes, that thing called culture.

I've recently completes a Diploma of Positive Psychology and Wellbeing. The reactions from some quarters are interesting, and at times all too predictable, when I tell people this. Let's just say, cue the eye-roll.

For anyone less familiar with Positive Psychology, you might be wondering what place does Positive Psychology have in workplace culture?

If you've got this far into the book, I'm guessing that either what you've done so far isn't working; your workplace is still a cot-case; you're miserable, disengaged and unhappy at work or maybe, just maybe, you're so fed up that you're thinking anything's gotta be better than this as a way to make a living.

Stick with me. There is a better way, I promise. And no fancy MBA, huge financial investment or massive change initiative is required. Hell, you could turn things around without even telling anyone what you're doing! Not only is it totally legit, it's scientifically proven (many times over), anyone with the desire to live a better life can do it and it's simple. It *does* require deliberate and intentional focus, attention and that old thing we touchy-feely types often talk about – an open mind (no weird woo-woo stuff, I promise!)

If you're still interested in having a vastly better life most of the time you're awake, whether you're the leader or one of the team, Millennial, Gen X-er or Boomer – then read on.

Positive Psychology at Work?

So, Positive Psychology. Let's dispel a few myths right now. What it isn't is some kind of flakey 'happiology', utopian, do-gooder, touchy-feely, latest fad, human resources initiative.

It's also not about people walking around smiling all the time, mindfully colouring in while reclining in bean bags in the common area, while they sip green tea, munch on quinoa salads and only talk about positive things. It's also *not* about ignoring, learning from or undervaluing negative feelings or events and the things that aren't working.

And, while it's great to have, a positive work environment has very little to do with the physical workspace, no matter how fabulous it is. (I once had a CEO say, 'We gave them a new fit-out, what more do they want?' Same person's response when shown his shocker employee engagement scores: 'That's just their perceptions'. Man oh man; some people really don't get it.)

What Positive Psychology is, is evidence-based science around human flourishing. It's about what makes us thrive and perform at the peak of our abilities – whatever they may be – and includes things like strengths, emotions, resilience, team dynamics, productivity, motivation and how these link to improved wellbeing.

Put simply, positivity or Positive Psychology is in part about catching people doing something right, focusing on what is working with people and the company in general, rather than overly or only focusing on what went wrong, who's to blame and how much will it cost.

Funny, as I was writing this at a writer's retreat, several of the other authors, knowing the theme of my book, came to talk to me about toxic cultures where they've worked. Wide-ranging workplaces too – hospitals, an airport, an optometrist's and a pharmaceutical company, a recruitment and an IT company, a couple of law firms, even a mental health unit. Sadly, all too common.

Have a go at asking the people around you now (that's if it's safe to bob your head up over the pod wall), how they feel about the culture where you work; ask your friends tonight, ask them at the pub or over the weekend. Good or bad, ask them what, specifically, makes the culture the way they've described. Then ask them how they'd feel if their current boss left.

Their answers, I promise you, will be very revealing on several fronts, and lead me to the next chapter. People who love their culture will generally tell you they'd be somewhat nervous about getting a new boss, particularly someone unknown. Others who're schlepping into work, fulfilling the requirements of their JD just to pay the bills, keeping their heads down to avoid getting the chop – they will very possibly express elation at the very thought of a new boss, one who it's safe to place in with the humans.

Here's another interesting Paleo-times fact. Back then, we were all built for speed more than comfort and, like animals, we didn't see exercise as some form of torture to be endured, but a way to survive. Our bodies are in effect built to be in constant motion (about twenty kilometres per day for the male of the species, and about twelve to fifteen for females) searching for food, with that exercise stimulating oxygen to feed our brains so we could deal with unforeseen problems and come up with creative solutions. If you want to shut down the human brain, stick it behind a desk or in a pod all day.

When Culture Thrives

So, what happens when you have a culture where people thrive? Is it necessary or even worth bothering about? And are the benefits really measureable?

Numerous studies and many years of research tell us that how people feel about working for a place, the culture or company climate, is unequivocally critical to hard results. Measureable results like profit, productivity, customer satisfaction and retention.

Still not sure? How about the research results from a sample size of four million people?

Tom Rath and Donald Clifton[5] of the Gallup Organisation studied the results of over 50 years' worth of comprehensive Gallup workplace research. Re-cutting the data Gallup had accumulated over these years, and comparing the results to financial results and other 'hard', measureable data, they came up with some pretty impressive figures, showing just how important are the previously so-called soft skills, now known as adaptive skills.

Companies that were reported as being better at the adaptive skills – recognition, a strengths-based culture and positive leadership – consistently showed the following improvements in hard results over those that were reported by employees as being not so good:

- Productivity *higher* by 22%

- Customer satisfaction *higher* by 38%

- Profit *higher* by 27%

- Retention *higher* by 22%

I'll give you a moment to let those numbers sink in …

They also found measureable increases in their individual employee's productivity, increased engagement and cross-functional collaboration (farewell to those silos), better safety records and fewer accidents on the job. People also stayed longer with these companies and they scored higher across several critical measures from customers such as brand loyalty and general satisfaction.

Throughout *Culture 101*, I'll be sharing a lot of research stats with you, stats like those above that are hard to argue

---

5 - *How Full is Your Bucket*, Tom Rath and Donald Clifton Gallup Press, 2004

with. Stats to help you take the first tentative steps towards creating a place where people thrive and your profit grows – as you'll see, a lot of these steps are well within your control and don't require budget. Most are about a shift in your mindset, about being focused, mindful (we'll talk more about mindfulness and no, it doesn't require loose pants and a yoga mat) in what you do, and maybe a bit of letting go. By the way, these stats will also help you to build a case with whoever needs case-building, to help you get buy-in or budget if you decide it's time to 'go big', or risk going down.

A Positive, Strengths-Based Culture

At the risk of putting you into a bit of a funk momentarily, can I get you to think back to your past performance reviews, performance appraisals, those bi-monthly, quarterly, annual one-to-ones with your manager where you talk about … well, what do you talk about? From what I read, from what people tell me, from more research, as well as from personal experience, these sessions appear, in the main, to be all about what's not working, your weaknesses and where you need to improve.

Very rarely have I had someone tell me that these sorts of sessions were life-changing, career-accelerating, thought-provoking, energising and something they always came away from with a spring in their step, a renewed sense of focus, purpose and enthusiasm about their job and the company itself.

What's the problem some may ask? People need to be aware of their weaknesses. Yep, no problem there. But let's take a look at the impact on productivity when people are *managed* to their weaknesses, and at the almost total exclusion of any discussion or development around their strengths. Then compare this type of all-too-common pattern with companies who focus on strengths.

Back in 1999, Marcus Buckingham[6] and his colleagues, also at the Gallup Organisation, used over 25 years of research to demonstrate that focusing on people's weaknesses not only had hairs on it, it had a profoundly negative impact on productivity and profitability. They urged leaders to shift to a culture focused on rewarding and developing people's strengths, if the company sought long-term sustainable improvement across all the core measures of thriving.

Scroll forward a few years and Alex Linley and his research team at CAPPfinity developed the Strengths Profile, a robust and well-validated tool that's been taken by over six million people worldwide.

Linley describes a strength as 'a pre-existing capacity for a particular way of behaving, thinking or feeling that is authentic and energising to the user, and enables optimal functioning, development and performance'.[7]

Here's some compelling numbers from CAPPfinity's comprehensive research study of 19,000 people in 34 organisations. They came up with a startling and unarguably important discovery in terms of what it might be costing a company and an employee to operate in a deficit-focused culture.

In organisations that managed people to or overly focused on weaknesses, from a baseline, **performance dropped by 26.8%**. By comparison, companies that focused on, managed and developed people to their strengths, **showed an increase in performance of 36.4%.**

Have a think for a moment about what it would be like as a kid in primary school, going in day after day and having the teacher only tell you what you sucked at and needed to improve. Thankfully, good teachers don't operate that way.

---

6 - *First Break all the Rules: What the Worlds' Greatest Managers Do Differently,* Marcus Buckingham and Curt Coffman, Simon & Schuster,1999
7 - *Average to A+: Realizing Strengths in Yourself and Others,* Alex Linley, Wiley, 2008

Think maybe they're on to something?

Overall, what have they found are the beneficial outcomes, personal and company wise, from adopting a positive, strengths-based focus?

A lot of stuff that matters, so it seems, to employees and employers, gets better. Things like achieving goals, even stretch goals, is easier and more efficient; individual productivity and energy levels are higher; people are sick less, report feeling better generally and are more engaged; discretionary effort is a given; innovation is easier; silos are a thing of the past and collaboration, even cross-functional collaboration, is smoother and if a change is coming through, people are more open to it and handle it better. Oh, and more resilience – people bounce back quicker from setbacks.

That's a pretty impressive list right there.

And, in case you think I'm living in la-la land, I haven't forgotten about those weaknesses that we all have and inevitably need to employ from time to time.

From Carl Jung way back at the beginning of last century right through to now, what science has shown us is this: as long as we can be ourselves, do what we love, what we're best at, use our strengths for about 70% to 75% of the time at work, we manage the rest, including those things that don't come naturally to us. This is the space where we adapt so we can get stuff done through and with others. It's where we rein in or marshal our strengths from time to time as appropriate. And it's an important aspect of being an adaptive leader.

How do we do that without killing the geese that are laying golden eggs for themselves and for the company?

Here's the simple, and I do mean simple, answer.

When people have a rock-solid, crystal clear, connected-to-my-values sense of meaning and purpose, have trustworthy, authentic leaders who demonstrate this meaning and purpose every day, and a company that *genuinely* cares about their wellbeing, then when 'duty calls' and people need to get on with something they're not great at, usually one of two things will happen.

Either people will draw on one of their strengths to get these things done, or, because positively led, strengths-based cultures foster great collaboration, they'll find a willing colleague to help, who has a strength where they're not so strong.

Positivity and Creativity, Hand in Glove

Finally, if you're stuck coming up with new, catalytic, miles-in-front-of-your-competitors, breakthrough ideas or products, then check out this little gem. Barbara Fredrickson[8], another key and very prolific researcher in the Positive Psychology space, developed the Broaden and Build theory to describe some of the important outcomes of a positive workplace culture. 'Positive emotions … open our hearts and minds, making us more receptive and creative … transforms us for the better … Positive emotions allow us to discover and build new skills, new ties, new knowledge and new ways of being.'

Imagine then, if you were working in a positive, thriving, strengths-based culture, where the goal is to have everyone working at their optimal level, feeling well and using their strengths every day. What would those one-to-one sessions be like now?

Enough stats for now, let's have a look at how to go about the business of creating a place where people thrive and profits grow, starting, you guessed it, at the top.

---

8 - *Positivity; Ground Breaking Research to Release Your Inner Optimist and Thrive*
Barbara Fredrickson, Oneworld, 2009

KEY TAKEAWAYS

- Positive Psychology is based on science about what makes people thrive and perform at their peak, and incorporates strengths, emotions, resilience, team dynamics, productivity and motivation.

- Companies with positive, strengths-based cultures consistently outperform those who don't on critical scores such as retention, customer satisfaction, productivity and profit.

- A positive culture leads to increased employee wellbeing.

- Managing individual performance based on strengths has been shown to lift productivity by 36.4%, compared to a decline of 28.6% where skills deficits were the focus.

- A positive culture impacts innovation by opening our minds to more ideas and building on those ideas.

REFLECTION QUESTIONS

- Where would you place your company in terms of innovation? Thought leaders, game changers, surfing the fringe? Or struggling to come up with new ideas, so you end up being a 'me two', me three or worse?

- How clear are you about your strengths and those of your team?

- Where are your engagement scores? How do these numbers align with your other results, good or not so good?

EARN THE RIGHT

- WHERE THE BUCK STOPS (AND STARTS)

- SO, REMIND ME, WHY EXACTLY ARE WE ALL HERE?

- THE GIFT OF YOUR ATTENTION

- WHAT'S THE STORY WITH TELLING STORIES AT WORK?

Chapter 3

WHERE THE BUCK STOPS (AND STARTS)

And what of him as a man? I recalled the way in which he had led his party across the ice-floes after the Endurance had been lost; how, by his genius for leadership he had kept us all in health; how, by the sheer force of his personality he had kept our spirits up; and how, by his magnificent example, he had enabled us to win through when the dice of the elements were loaded most heavily against us ... He was a proud and dauntless spirit, a spirit that made one glad he was an Englishman. Surely there is no end with such a man as Shackleton: something of his spirit must still live on with us; something of his greatness must surely be a legacy to his countrymen. 'He had a way of compelling loyalty,' writes one who sailed with him. 'We would have gone anywhere without question just on his order.' What more glowing tribute could any man wish for?

Eulogy for Sir Ernest Shackleton, from Frank Worsley, Captain of the Endurance [9]

---

9 - *Leadership in Crisis: Ernest Shackleton and the Epic Voyage of the Endurance;*

Anyone reading the quote above who's been to some of my leadership workshops will likely be chuckling right now. I am, you see, a vocal and very passionate advocate of the great Sir Ernest Shackleton, and in most of my leadership workshops I play a key segment of the Sir Kenneth Branagh BBC Shackleton series. I've even had the hilarious participants in one group (you know who you are!) take bets on how many times I'd mention him in a follow up presentation. That's how much I revere him.

Why do I revere this legend of a man? To me, he embodies much of what positive leadership is all about, the type of leadership that creates and fosters a culture of personal and company success, deep accountability, team commitment, innovation, thriving and wellbeing.

What Shackleton is most renowned for is that he never lost a man on any of his explorations, the most famous of these being the doomed trip in 1915 on the ship *Endurance*. For those less familiar with the story, the *Endurance* became stuck in pack ice in the Weddell Sea in Antarctica on January 18, 1915 where it stayed stuck until October 28, 1915. That was the day that Shackleton had to make the heartbreaking and frankly terrifying decision to abandon ship as she was crushed by the pack ice.

No Gore-Tex coats, no mobile phones or Satnav, no Arctic-rated down sleeping bags, no Cat skidoos, no chance of rescue – zip, nada, nothing. And yet, because of the way he led and treated his men, the legacy of leadership, discipline and morale he left when he and a small group had to leave 22 of the crew to go and find help, and despite the unbelievably enormous odds stacked against them, every single person survived for four whole months, until he came back to rescue them.

When I turn the lights up after showing the 15-minute segment in the series, without exception there's a sort of

---

Nancy Koehn, Harvard Business Review December 2, 2010.

hushed reverential silence as people contemplate and digest what they just saw in terms of leadership and dealing with extreme challenges. At one of the leadership gigs I ran, one of the group broke that silence by saying, 'Well, so what, he didn't have P & L to manage'. Once the laughter and guffawing had subsided – I did manage to contain myself – I pointed out that he did indeed have financial concerns. He'd begged, borrowed, cajoled and schmoozed people all over Britain, including the King and the Royal Geographical Society, to fund the trip. So yes buddy, on top of no creature comforts, he had people back in the old dart waiting for him to cough up on his return.

If you have a chance to, and want to get some perspective on how challenging your leadership problems are right now, take a look at the series. One of the reasons I love it and use it in my programs (and the reason my bucket list includes a visit to his grave in Antarctica) is because the BBC based the series on the journal entries of the men from the Endurance, whose lives he saved through his exemplary leadership. Not some Hollywood puffball with a happy ending, but the real deal, down to the actual words spoken by Shackleton and others.

You see, right from the get-go, when Shackleton was recruiting for the trip (have a read of the HBR article) and based on his previous experiences in Antarctica with Sir Robert Falcon Scott, he spoke of the need to find the right type of people with different strengths, a hell of a lot of resilience and traits that would give them all the best chance of succeeding in their venture to conquer the South Pole.

'Shackleton looked for qualities he associated with optimism, a personal trait he felt was essential for men undertaking a potentially dangerous and difficult mission. Those who displayed cheerfulness and a sense of humour tended to fare well in interviews with him.'[10]

---

10 - *Leadership in Crisis: Ernest Shackleton and the Epic Voyage of the Endurance;*

And, as a powerful testimony to his leadership and of the esteem in which his men held him, many of the *Endurance* crew went on to follow him on a subsequent expedition.

Becoming the Boss

Once you've got the promotion, the real work of leading a thriving culture begins. Sadly though, in company after company, promotion into leadership roles, frequently leading your former peers, can be a slippery slope from top gun to lacklustre leadership, and too often goes something like this:

You've been in your job for a while now; you've kicked goals, hit targets, achieved objectives, innovated and created. You're one of the best, maybe the stand-out best, at whatever it is you do – finance, IT, sales, customer service, HR etc. And so, you get offered a promotion into a leadership role. Depending on the size and type of your company, you're about to become, for example, a team leader, supervisor, section leader, general manager or state manager.

Fabulous! Congratulations! You head home on Friday night after a couple of celebratory drinks with your workmates, having noticed an odd, slightly uneasy feeling as they chatted to you. And, as you fill in the requisition form for the new, shiny, bigger car to go with the new shiny, bigger job, it hits you. You're now their boss. And as most leaders will tell you, this is one of the toughest transitions to make.

If you're lucky you've been on some kind of emerging leaders program and, if you're luckier still, have had a coach or mentor to prepare you for this incredible transition in your career. Sadly, all too many people have been left to wing it, hoping for and desperately trying to do their best.

Either way, your journey as a leader starts now. Now is the time to start thinking about the legacy you'd like to leave,

---

Nancy Koehn, Harvard Business Review December 2, 2010

whether that's for the next person into the role after you, when you leave the company or when you retire.

Yes, there are a few balls in the air now, lots of balancing and reordering. One of the most common questions I get asked is how to balance leading and managing people, with the results or profit side of the business. My answer is always this – fundamentally, the main thing is that if you get the people and culture stuff right, the productivity and profit will follow. Funny that.

The hardest thing though, for most people, is in starting to let go of the relative security of your technical skills. You know, those wonderful skills you've honed and developed, that led to your track record of success and excellence, and then led to you being offered the leadership gig. Because the fact is that the higher up the leadership ladder you go, the more critical people and culture related skills become. And while being busy doing tech skills stuff might appear to be what you need to do, that way does not success and profitability guarantee.

Remembering that there's no place for ego in leadership, this is when you need to get very savvy about delegating things, too. Things to stretch people below you, things someone can do more economically or better than you, things you just don't have time to do.

Earning the right is everything now if you want to have what's called informal authority – where people will do what you ask of them not just because of your title, but because you've earned the right. And they'll do those things even when you're not there – another true mark of leadership.

Culture – Ground Zero

If you want to see a room full of people go quiet, ask them this question: 'Who's the best boss you've ever had and why?'

With any luck, one or two will wistfully share their story of the great person who is or was that leader who helped them shine, who they'd happily go the extra mile for, who drew out the best in them and who led the team to continuing success.

Back in my days as a social worker, I worked under one of the finest leaders I've ever had. He exemplified everything that *Culture 101* is about, and though he did do an MBA a few years later, without apparently having had any specific leadership training when I worked with him, he was everything you'd want in a leader. He got to know each and every one of us and knew what made us tick; he quietly oversaw many outstanding individual achievements (never taking the credit); inspired great confidence (so much so in me, that in a doctor-oriented-organisation first, I negotiated for and secured financial assistance for a non-medical person to attend and present a paper at an international conference – unheard of!), and fierce loyalty from our mixed bag of health professionals. He always had our backs, even in tough situations with senior medicos; he pushed us out of our comfort zones and supported us when the proverbial hit the fan. We're still friends to this today, a few decades later.

The truth of the matter is that the buck really does start and stop with the leader. There's an old saying, attributed to various sources, that sums up the impact of leadership on culture: 'The fish stinks from the head'. Harsh I know, but sometimes a bit of a slap across the face with a wet (and stinky) fish is what people need to wake up and smell the reality of what your culture's become.

Bucket loads of research from Daniel Goleman[11] and others tell us what multiple climate and engagement surveys reflect – the leader in any team or group is what drives the

---

11 - *Primal Leadership: Unleashing the Power of Emotional Intelligence*, Professor Daniel Goleman PhD, Richard Boyatzis, Annie McKee

culture, how people feel about working at a company, and can account for 20% to 30% of productivity and profitability. And that's 20% to 30%, up or down.

The leader's mood you see is highly infectious and the team will take their emotional cue from the boss. If Shackleton had walked around looking glum, hopeless and defeated, it's highly unlikely he and his men would have survived. I'm not talking about being Pollyanna here, what I am talking about is what I call realistic optimism, even when the chips are down.

During tough times, that might sound something like this: 'I know things look bad right now, it might be hard to see a way ahead. I don't know what the answers are, but what I do know is that we have a great team here and we've weathered some tough times before. Let's get our heads together and smash out some ideas'. Realistic optimism, that's what I call it.

Red Socks (not the Boston ones)

As Sue Langley, CEO of The Langley Group, says, 'When you become the leader, you may need to ask yourself some hard questions. For instance, do you energise a room more when you walk in to it, or when you walk out of it?'. Becoming aware of your emotional wake and its impact is a key element of positive leadership.

Bottom line is, with everyone taking their cue from you now you're the leader, you're ground zero when it comes to creating a culture where people thrive and profits grow. Your choice. You'll either be Typhoid Mary or you'll be the Shackelton at your place who makes things possible, lifts morale and kicks the energy up a few notches – even when the chips are down.

Some years ago, I had the good fortune to hear the managing director of one of our largest health insurers talk at a conference where I was about to present.

One of the subjects he covered was around how absolutely critical it is to make sure you have the right people in your teams – people who lift a team up, inject it with energy and ideas, share the load and generally leave people in a better head space when they depart. *Not* the kind of people, regardless of their role, seniority or how much income they bring into the company, who bring the team and everyone around it down, regularly and with serious and costly side effects.

He used the analogy of what happens when you put a red sock in with your washing by mistake. As most of us will know from unfortunate experience, it will 'taint' everything in the wash, rendering some things damaged beyond use.

Which, regrettably, is exactly what happens if you have a 'red sock' in a team and fail to deal with the person appropriately. Their negativity, criticism and general bad attitude infects everyone they come into contact with, and, particularly if they're in a senior position, the 'infection' can be widespread and very costly.

And it will inevitably have a direct impact on your customers and your profits.

In David Hamilton's book, *The Contagious Power of Thinking*[12], he quotes research covering around 50,000 customers of about 2000 employees of a large retail chain. He notes that 'the moods of leaders are so contagious that they actually affect the bottom line … for each 1 point decrease in a manager's job satisfaction (and general attitude), there was a 5% decrease in customer spending'.

When you do a few numbers, that's one big heap of income lost, on a daily basis, for good.

Often, in fact a bit too often, people tell me that they see the 'red sock' being tolerated, with 'infectious' behaviour being

---

12 - *The Contagious Power of Thinking*, Dr. David Hamilton, Hay House, 2011

condoned, largely because they are the biggest income producer, or are in a senior role. Yet, if you do the numbers it should become abundantly clear what the *real* cost is to the company of allowing the 'red sock' to continue infecting people left, right and centre.

In Chapter 10, I'll look at how you can start to manage the 'deep and meaningful fireside chat' you probably need to have with these sorts of people. Unfortunately perhaps, a challenge left behind by someone who lacked the know-how, or frankly the courage, to deal with the red sock you've now inherited. Great legacy ...

Breaking the Grip of a Bad Day

Given you're human, the reality is that there are going to be days when, for whatever reason, you're not in top form, it's a bit harder to put on your game face and you'd rather be anywhere but at work under the spotlight gaze of your boss and team.

Rather than become some wooden version of yourself, walking around with a fake smile plastered on your face, here are a couple of simple things you can do if you're having a bad day, if in fact you're just being human – and this isn't about wearing your heart on your sleeve, pouring your woes out to your team or slamming the door and shutting yourself away from people. All of which will serve to dig a bit of a hole that may be hard to drag yourself out of over time.

I can promise you that in the absence of any realistic explanation from you, over time the team will start to fill in the gaps with their own version of reality, when they see you in a less than ideal mood.

Here's a bit of important info on that fake smile. Picture for a moment the late, great Nelson Mandela. In most pictures of him that I see, he is wearing a smile, a warm, welcoming, genuine smile. Hold that thought.

When you smile, I mean really smile, there's a bucket load of good stuff that happens in your brain, and in the brains of others who see you smile. These types of smiles have a name – the Duchenne smile (who knew - a smile with its own name!), and you might just find yourself rethinking the Botox after you read what's coming up!

A Duchenne smile is when your face really crinkles up, your mouth curves up and your eyes get involved, with those little muscles at the sides of your eyes joining in to the face party – yes, those muscles that give you crow's feet. Shocker of a name for something fabulous, as you're about to find out. The fake smiles on the other hand are just a turn up of the corners of the mouth – no crinkly eyes, and no message to your own or anyone else's brain that you're happy. It's also not physiologically possible to do the crow's feet muscle crinkle voluntarily without smiling (…and I know you just tried to didn't you!)

Duchenne smiles are truly incredible. They're free, anyone can do them at any time and they have an immediate positive impact, even if you're not in the best mental space to start with. Because, you see, your brain doesn't know if you're faking it 'til you make it, or are in fact smiling because you're already happy.

When you slap on one of these fabulous smiles, your brain, which is basically sitting on idle, waiting on commands from ground control, gets a message that you're happy and so it releases a neurotransmitter called endorphins, basically your personal supply of a morphine-like substance and serotonin, your personal supply of a get-happy hormone. The endorphin and serotonin hits in turn, then make you feel really happy, and, as a side effect, also lowers your stress levels. (As I'm writing this, I'm grinning from ear to ear and crinkling up my eyes – I need the endorphin and serotonin hit to get the book to the publisher on time. You can see why I love neuroscience!)

If you haven't already, make it your business to know and build your EI (or EQ – emotional intelligence) muscles. Your every move and mood is now the subject of much scrutiny and discussion. You're not being measured so much on your technical skills now as on your personal style, and that can be hard to take on board if you've been blissfully unaware of your impact on others. Get familiar with what might affect your mood, up or down, so you're in the driving seat, so you can plan for how you'll deal with button-pushing people and situations (of course, once you've put in place the suggestions in *Culture 101*, you'll should start to find that your buttons, and other peoples', are far less likely to be pushed with such monotonous regularity).

A great way to do this is to use an app called How We Feel created by a team of scientists, designers, engineers, and therapists in collaboration with the **Yale Center for Emotional Intelligence.** It's a four-quadrant tool divided into red, blue, green, and yellow quadrants. Each quadrant relates to a different set of feelings, grouped together based on how pleasant or not it is and what it does to your energy level, and tips on how to shift to a more helpful mood – kinda like having a coach in your pocket.

Tips to Shift a Not-So-Great Mood

- Name the emotion to yourself – Just naming out loud how you're feeling takes away the emotion and reduces any possible amygdala involvement. And yes, probably in the car, before you start the engine, or in the shower.

- Use the How We Feel app to build awareness of your moods and to see any patterns

- Be open with your team, at a high level – If it's appropriate, tell people what you can, not spill-your-guts stuff, just enough so they're not left wondering. Name the emotion to them, even if it sounds something like, 'Hey team, just letting you know I may look a bit out of sorts for a couple days, my cat passed away'.

* Duchenne smile – Fake it 'til you make it. I defy you to stay in a foul mood while wearing a Duchenne smile.

Change Your Expectations, Change Your Culture, Change Your Results

Remember I promised that the ideas and tools in *Culture 101* would be easy to implement, no huge budget or expensive further education required? Remember also that I said it does require deliberate and intentional focus, self-awareness and commitment?

As mentioned, as the leader, science tells us that what you say and what you think is very contagious when you're the boss.

The **Pygmalion Effect**[13] is a type of self-fulfilling prophecy where if you think something will happen, you may unconsciously make it happen through your actions or your inaction. Professor Dov Eden has done research on the Pygmalion Effect across diverse industry sectors and job types. What his research shows is that if the boss has an expectation of, for example, good or bad financial results or of individual underperformance, surprise, surprise, it pretty much comes true.

So, here's something else you can do right now to start on the journey to a thriving culture. Professor Dov Eden and his team found that by holding positive expectations of people, for example, ***genuinely*** believing that your team or an individual can solve a challenging problem, people perform better. Conversely, the same applies if the leader has pessimistic expectations. Negative leader expectation leads to poor performance, called The Golem Effect. *'The*

---

13 - Named after George Bernard Shaw's play in which a professor, Henry Higgins transforms a simple street flower seller into a lady because he believes it can be done

bottom line is this: Leaders, believe in your team. Hold positive and high expectations that they will solve that difficult problem, meet the seemingly insurmountable challenge and, more often than not, they will meet or exceed your expectations'.[14]

The reason I've emphasised genuinely is simple. You or someone else in your position employed these people, I'm assuming because their strengths fit the job requirements, and they're intelligent people who want to succeed – that's human nature and a key driver of motivation. So, I'm assuming you're reading *Culture 101* because you have a genuine desire to see them and your company thrive.

This is how the Pygmalion Effect might look:

Leader with Positive Expectations of a Team Member

- Gives high levels of autonomy

- Sees mistakes as a learning opportunity

- Offers appropriate level of support and makes self available whenever needed

- Shows genuine interest in team members' suggestions and ideas

- Allocates interesting stretch projects aligned with team members' strengths

- Collaborates with team members on strategic and company-wide initiatives

- Offers unsolicited positive feedback and praise

- Asks for and may defer to team members' opinion in difference-of-opinion situations

---

14 - *Being Honest About the Pygmalion Effect*, Discover Magazine December 2015

Leader with Negative Expectations of a Team Member

- Is highly directive and micro-managing

- Sees mistakes as proof of incompetence and refers to them constantly

- Only available for formal one to one pre-arranged support

- Shows little interest in any suggestions or ideas from team members

- Gives routine, boring projects, often well below the scope of team members' area of strength

- Rarely, if ever, asks for input on strategic and company-wide initiatives

- Gives only negative feedback; focused on catching team member doing something wrong

- Doesn't listen to or solicit team members' perspective in situations of conflict or disagreement

This is not to say that sometimes people are simply never going to work out in the role in your company that they're in. In some cases though, someone has to start building a bridge and that someone is you, giving people a chance, using all the relevant resources in *Culture 101*. People will make their own choice about whether they choose to build the bridge from their side.

Trust – A Small Word Punching Above Its Weight

Some years ago, I had the great joy of singing at the Sydney Opera House. Not quite Adele or Dame Nellie Melba, but I was part of the massed choir singing Handel's Messiah with the Sydney Philharmonic Choir and Philharmonic Orchestra.

Prior to this, when I'd watched orchestras being conducted, I thought to myself, 'What a great gig! Stand up there in your tux, wave a stick around and get paid a lot of money!' Too easy!

Boy, was I wrong, as I came to find out.

In the weeks leading up to the performances, we met for practice in various parts of Sydney, eventually meeting as one big choir for dress rehearsals with the professional choir and the orchestra as well as the conductor. At one rehearsal, before the orchestra joined us, I noticed the conductor going around the orchestra pit with his score, stopping at music stands in front of various instruments – the lead violin, cellos, oboe and a couple of others. As he stopped in front of each music stand, he stood silently looking at his score, looking at that instrument player's score and then he made notes and small changes to their individual scores. I was blown away.

What he was doing was playing that piece of the entire orchestral and vocal score in his head, zeroing in on the part of that instrument and its player, and making slight changes to achieve a better overall sound. Clearly with a deep understanding of the part each person in that orchestra played to achieve the best performance. Genius.

And it didn't stop there.

Let me paint the picture for you. As the performance was about to begin, the conductor had about 600 people looking down from the choir stalls at him. He, of course, was alone on that little podium with his back to the audience of about 4000 people. Noise travels forward and out of course, so he was the only one who could hear the whole sound, hence we were all totally reliant on trusting him to gently wave that seemingly innocuous little stick in our direction when it was time for each section of the choir to join in.

I'm an alto and, for anyone who knows Handel's Messiah, after the overture we're the first to sing. Not wanting to make a fool of myself by peaking too soon, I was so focused on that hand holding the baton that time fell away. I was sweating bullets; the conductor was cool as a cucumber. And then … that gentle wave of the baton and off we went.

It was one of the most exhilarating experiences of my life and one of the most profound yet simple examples of leadership. He knew every note of every part of that incredible piece of music, played and sung by each person there. And without being able to trust him, to know he'd lead us through the entire performance to a successful outcome – well, let's just say my singing days would've ended there along those of a few other budding musos.

In many of my leadership programs, I ask people to think of a leader we'd all know, living or not, who they admire, who each person in the group sees as representative of outstanding leadership and then to jot down three words or phrases to describe what makes them a great leader. Interestingly, in survey after survey, people around the globe have been asked similar questions in terms of what they look for in a leader. The top four traits everyone comes up with? Trust comes in at number one, followed by compassion, stability and hope.

Trust: a small word punching above its weight to cover a pretty hefty topic.

Neuroeconomics professor Paul Zak and his team came up with some startling figures in their research on just how important a culture of trust is to your bottom line. *'Compared with people at low-trust companies, people at high-trust companies report 74% less stress, 106% more energy at work, 50% higher productivity, 13% fewer sick days, 76% more engagement, 29% more satisfaction with their lives and 40% less burnout – high-trust companies hold people accountable but without micromanaging them. They treat people like responsible adults'.* [15]

Those are some mighty fine figures right there, just for being trustworthy.

In short, to be the kind of leader who fosters a thriving culture, there are a few things to get right and to keep getting right, ideally from the get-go.

Mistakes, I've Made A few …

Authentic leadership. From time to time, I've had people tell me that they struggle with the idea of being an authentic leader. What does it mean? Is it about wearing your heart on your sleeve? How do I know I'm being authentic?

Be wary, very wary, of a couple of big mistakes I made when I stepped into leadership roles. And I'm not alone, by a long stretch. I made two huge, very common mistakes.

Firstly, I thought I had to be ten-foot tall, bullet-proof, perfect from day one, please everyone and have all the answers. And secondly, I started trying to be like everyone else at my level, striving to apply some cookie-cutter image of what the perfect leader looked, sounded and operated like. Leaving my wonderful, authentic self in the car park, along with most of my individual strengths, some of my values, and at times what felt like my brain, as I tried to negotiate the shadowy corridors of a couple of highly political, catch 'em doing something wrong, numbers are everything, set up to fail, people are dispensable cultures.

Whether you're a new manager or a seasoned traveller, the number one thing to do, if you haven't done it already, is to get to know yourself, really, really, really well. (Any of the many books on emotional intelligence will tell you that self-

---

15 - *The Neuroscience of Trust*, Paul J. Zak, Harvard Business Review January February 2017

awareness is the number one trait or competency to foster to become more emotionally intelligent).

Get to know your strengths, where your potential lies, the things you're not so good at and the impact you have on other people. Get very clear on your values using something like the Values in Action survey, and make sure that there's a seamless transition between your values at home and at work.

Why are authenticity and alignment of yours and your peoples' values so important to success, personal and company-wide?

Have you ever been gob-smacked at discovering someone you worked with, or some high-profile mover and shaker (or a whole group of them), had committed large-scale fraud? Had maybe cheated to the tune of multiple seven figures? Perhaps turned a blind eye to mistakes with devastating implications such as catastrophic environmental damage? People who at home are pillars of society?

As Margaret Heffernan noted in the March 2005 issue of FastCompany, *'Many corporate cultures ... lead to people compartmentalizing their lives ... a work self ... and a true self, carefully locked away from each other'. This kind of splitting, psychologists will tell you, has a bad reputation. Once you split off part of yourself, what's left rules without checks or balances.*

'It can come as no real surprise that when one investigates the lives of many criminals – white collar and war criminals alike – the integration of their work and home lives is strikingly absent. The problem with compartmentalization, it turns out, is that it offers its proponents the opportunity to lie. It helps good people to do bad things ...

'And yet compartmentalization is a characteristic, even a requirement, of so many corporate cultures ... 24-hour deal negotiations, all-nighters ... punishing schedules, endless travel

and repeated relocations for example … teach you tolerance for leaving your private values in the car. In cultures like these, it can come as no surprise when executives lose their sense of right and wrong: they were trained to lock it away. If we take our whole selves to work, we can transform the culture and sustain ourselves'.

In short, Heffernan sends a very strong and disturbing message about what can happen when you leave your true self behind.

In the following chapters, I'll share some simple yet powerful ideas, information and tools you can use, framed around the **FOUR KEYS TO CULTURE**, the areas to focus on as you go about building your thriving team and a company culture of success.

There are also resources you can access to help make it through in one piece, knowing that you're contributing to a culture where people can thrive and profits will grow, and being confident in the knowledge that people will say great stuff about you when you're no longer there.

And The Four Keys to Culture?

EARNING THE RIGHT – People won't trust you or allow you to influence them just because you want them to. This is the work of clarifying the purpose of the company and each person's part in contributing to that purpose, and continuing to create a thriving culture, step-by-step, person-by-person.

ACHIEVEMENT, PRODUCTIVITY AND PROFITABILITY – This is the outcome of the culture you're creating with your team and if you earn the right, and keep on earning it, this will be soooooo much easier.

COACHING AND MENTORING – Remember those things that people look for at work? Help them to clarify and use their strengths so they're in a success loop; coach them through finding their own answers and share your wisdom and knowledge judiciously when they're really stuck with the tough stuff.

LEAVE A LEGACY OF WELLBEING – What shape do you want to leave people in when you go? What do you want people, your team, your peers and your clients to say about you when you're gone? Are you going to leave things in good shape or a mess for someone else to inherit and sort out?

Chapter 4

SO, REMIND ME, WHY EXACTLY ARE WE ALL HERE?

When people are financially invested, they want
a return. When people are emotionally invested,
they want to contribute.

Simon Sinek

S ome years ago, referred by another client, I went in to
meet with the AsiaPac managing partner of one of the
world's largest law firms. They had, as it turned out, a real
shocker of a culture problem.

For starters, turnover across the board was at a massive
50%. They were rapidly recruiting new grads to fill the spots
left by the young associates who themselves had joined as
grads two years prior (interesting strategy that, kind of
like giving someone a blood transfusion but neglecting to
do anything about the gaping, bleeding wound), as well
as poaching lawyers from competitor firms. The young
graduate associates I was told, were generally the 'gophers'
in the firm – they did all the hack-work, go for this, go for

that, at the beck and call of the more senior lawyers. Okay, problem number one was huge turnover – that's a clue. So, what else was going on?

Behaviour that I can only describe as, frankly, unhinged, was essentially being condoned from the top down. We're talking unfettered, crazy, frightening, dangerous, lock-them-in-a-padded-cell-and-throw-away-the-key kind of crazy. Throwing law books at people (have you seen the *size* of those bad boys?), ripping out phones (pre-mobiles folks, these were phones that were tethered to the walls or floor via cables) and throwing them at people, kicking in doors, smashing furniture, hanging junior associates out to dry to take the blame for the seniors' mistakes and oversights, screaming, swearing, clench-fisted, spittle-at-the-corner-of-the-mouth type of behaviour.

Why unfettered? Because the lawyers engaged in this appalling behaviour were the 'big billers' bringing in the big bucks from major clients. And if you've ever watched *Suits* or *The Good Wife*, well, you've seen what happens when you pee off a big billing lawyer. Off they go to your biggest competitor taking those lucrative clients with them.

The upshot of all this behaviour, leading to the massive turnover, was that the partners, those folks at the top of the pile who earned a tidy seven figures, were actually having to, as the managing partner called it, 'do law work'. This was, apparently, the law firm equivalent of Lady Bridgerton having to clean the toilets.

(At about this point, I was thinking that they possibly needed the police and a flock of psychiatrists more than my services. I had also noted where the emergency exits were, just in case …)

However, I pressed on hoping I could maybe save the day, make a difference, if I could just find a way in. I did used to be a social worker – helping is my second name. Thinking about the wonderful lawyers and barristers I know and have had the privilege of working with, I had an 'a-ha' moment – the aforementioned fabulous legal eagles I knew were all people who had a strong streak of altruism, fairness, wanting to see justice done. They all had and still have a strong sense of meaning and purpose. I was on to something!

So, I asked the question, 'What's the core purpose of the firm?'

The answer? 'To make money.'

If I could, I'd insert the goggle-eyed emoji right here in this book.

Make money? Make money? MAKE MONEY? That, my friends, as you no doubt know, is an outcome, *not* a core purpose.

And, as Dan Pink[16] so aptly said, 'When the profit motive becomes unmoored from the purpose motive, bad things happen'. Bad things, indeed.

Needless to say, I walked away from what would have been a lucrative six-figure gig. My core purpose is what this book's about. Not money. Within the year, the firm that I'd been to had been taken over by another firm.

Jim Collins and Jerry Porras'[17] research showed that companies that are driven by purpose outperform those that aren't by a factor of 15:1. And even when the purpose driven companies suffered setbacks – markets, situations and customers can and do change – they got back on track quickly and moved forward again.

So, let's look at this core purpose, this meaning at work thing and why it's so critical to culture, to thriving and to being successful.

---

16 - *Drive: The Surprising Truth About What Motivates Us*, Dan Pink, Riverhead Books, 2008
17 - *Built to Last: Successful Habits of Visionary Companies*, Jim Collins and Jerry Porras, Harper Business, 2004

Trust, Meaning, Purpose and Profit

'The purpose of a business, then, must be explicit and go beyond boosting the share price or fulfilling some bland mission statement. People want to believe that they're part of something meaningful. The sense of purpose doesn't have to be grandiose or revolutionary, merely credible and anchored in values.'[18]

I talked a bit about trust in the previous chapter. And, just like you can't be a little bit pregnant, you can't be a little bit trustworthy as an individual or an organisation.

If it isn't already, the focus on building and sustaining trust must become part of your DNA if you want your people to thrive and your profits to grow. Maybe you've stepped in to a new role and realised you've been handed a poisoned chalice; maybe, trying to keep everyone happy, you've rashly made promises you couldn't or didn't keep; maybe you've overlooked one too many elephants in the room or it's been a case of do as I say not as I do.

Hold that thought for a moment and let's take a little side journey off into one of my favourite places – neuroscience. Nothing too taxing, just a quick look at a fabulous little hormone called oxytocin, often referred to as the 'tend and befriend' hormone.

If you've ever been pregnant or read about pregnancy, you may have heard of it (stick with me here, I promise it's not going to get weird). Briefly, it's one of the most potent and powerful of our hormones and directly affects our behaviour towards others. In the case of new parents, it's the stuff that starts the bonding with your new baby (plus kicking off some other great physiological things in mum that we won't go into here).

---

18 - *Another Day, Another Mountain to Climb* Margaret Heffernan, FastCompany, March 2005

Now, back into the world of meaning and purpose. Various experiments show that having a strong sense of direction, meaning and purpose actually stimulates the production of oxytocin – and so does trust! (Told you that little five-letter word works hard!) So, these two culture-critical things, working in a culture of trust and where the meaning and purpose of the company is clear, kind of feed off and reinforce each other leading to a little thing that Paul Zak and a few other science boffins[19] call 'joy'. Something I'm certain we could all do with a bit more of daily.

And guess what else can stimulate this amazing tend and befriend hormone? Paul Zak and his team found that the mere act of a leader showing a litte bit of vulnerability and asking for help, rather than constantly giving orders, actually causes oxytocin to kick in thereby building trust, which in turns frees up our minds to be more productive.

Love it! No fancy MBA required here folks, no swatting over dusty leadership books, a no-brainer really – though it is of course your wonderful brain doing its thing. And which is why I'll later get into the importance of asking questions, and the right kind of questions.

What's *Your* Purpose?

Looking for some fundamental change, crucial shifts in productivity or critical new behaviour change in people? Terrific – just shoot off an email, whip up a PowerPoint presentation or draw up a memo, right?

WRONG!

In Alan Deutschman's aptly named book *Change or Die*[20], he quotes research from Dr Edward Miller, then dean of the medical school and CEO of the hospital at Johns Hopkins

---

19 - *The Neuroscience of Trust*, Paul J. Zak, Harvard Business Review, January/
February 2017
20 - *Change or Die*, Alan Deutschman, HarperBusiness, 2007

University. Dr Miller's research, first shared at an IBM conference in 2004, found that only one in ten people change their lifestyle after major coronary-artery bypass surgery.

If you've seen what someone looks like after this surgery, well, let's just say hit by a bus comes close. And, apparently, it feels about the same.

So, just stop for a moment and think about what Dr Miller and his team of researchers found. What it means is that even with *premature death* as a motivator, 90% of people still don't make any lifestyle changes!

So, good luck with that email!

What did work, the researchers found, was working with the recovering patients on *WHY* they might want to make some much-needed changes to their lifestyle, something that grounded the changes, every day, in a sense of meaning, joy and purpose.

When the rehab team did this with patients the at times challenging lifestyle changes started to kick in.

One of the first things I get people to do when I'm career coaching is to send them off with a task to complete before we meet again. The task, using a framework and information that I give them, is to come back with their own simple, one to two sentence core purpose statement.

Some of these people are senior executives responsible for defining the vision, mission and strategies for various companies they've worked for. Yet regrettably few, if any, had ever considered this might be a good thing to do for themselves. We are all, after all, CEO's of our own lives; regardless of what job we might hold in an organisation.

Warning them that when they come up with it, it may sound hokey, or a a bit 'fluffy', I share my own personal mission statement, along with those of a few high-profile people.

Mine is, 'helping people find the magic in themselves' – which translates to the corporate by-line you see on my website or business card, Switch On Potential. Same thing really, but it doesn't light me up, or others for that matter it seems, unlike the from-the-heart statement about magic.

Steve Jobs' personal mission statement was, 'To make a contribution to the world by making tools for the mind that advance humankind'. Oprah Winfrey's: 'To be a teacher, and to be known for inspiring my students to be more than they thought they could be'.

As one wag put it, on being asked to do this, 'Oh, so you've gone all mung bean on me have you, now you want me to go on a journey to the centre of my navel'. Not quite, but it is just as vital to your wellbeing if you want to thrive and if you want your company to be successful.

Not to put too fine a point on it, your core purpose statement informs *everything* you do. It might change a bit over time, you might tweak it around the edges, but your core purpose statement will be your anchor, your rock, your go-to 'oracle' even. And believe me, it will give you far greater confidence in making decisions, especially if they're difficult or ambiguous.

Not sure about something you've been asked to do, or a new job, even if they're waving a big six or seven figure number at you? Check in with your core purpose.

Harvard professor Tal Ben-Shahar[21] says, '*We want to know that our actions have an actual effect, not just that we feel that they do … To live a meaningful life, we must have a **self-generated** purpose that possesses **personal significance** rather than one that is dictated by society's standards and expectations … in accordance with our own values and passions*'.

---

21 - *Happier,* Tal Ben-Shahar, McGraw- Hill, 2009

When it comes to a company core purpose, things don't change. A rock solid, well understood, daily lived and embraced core purpose helps everyone, from the bottom up, to make even the toughest of decisions. It shifts the focus from an internal, it's-all-about-us, all-about-making-money focus to an external, connected-to-something-bigger-than-ourselves focus.

It's the anchor that informs *everything* your people do and one of the big things that comes up time and again in engagement survey after engagement survey, regardless of generation. People are looking for a company that's got a clear sense of meaning and purpose, beyond just making money (I'm sure by now you can see where I'm going with this – money is the outcome, not the purpose).

If you can provide relatable, easy to understand examples of what the core purpose of your company might look like, even in ambiguous situations (more about this in Chapter 6), autonomy, real autonomy, happens. A nice side effect of which is that you'll be freed up to keep building your thriving culture.

Because *you'll know*, having earned the right by being crystal clear about the purpose of the company and your own purpose, that every person will link their actions, their behaviour and their decisions to your company's core purpose.

While doing some work with the emerging and current leaders at one of Australia's largest agribusiness companies, the topic of meaning and purpose came up every now and then.

This company is one I absolutely love working with for a variety of reasons. Apart from the down-to-earth people I meet across this wide, brown land that is Australia, I don't think I've ever come across such consistently passionate people. Many of them come from farming and agricultural backgrounds and often talked about what it's like when you're talking to customers, people who've been on the land for many years.

During a particularly difficult time during the company's long history, a group I was working with got chatting about the meaning and purpose of the company. One of the 'aggros' (agronomists – for anyone less familiar with the Aussie tradition of shortening words), looking somewhat despondent, said that really all she did was go out and test soil.

A few others chimed in with comments like, 'Yeah, all I do is trade wool/sell fertilizer/sell land etc. … '

As we discussed this in the group, what we eventually got to is that this company is essentially all about working with farmers to make sure that current and future generations can feed and clothe themselves.

Pretty noble purpose, I'd say; one the group totally connected with and which created quite a positive shift in the energy in the room.

(If you want to get a real sense of the challenges farmers deal with around the world, take a look at the YouTube clip of the RAM Trucks 2013 Super Bowl Ad. I still get a bit choked up when I watch it. Tough, tough gig.)

Defining Your Core Purpose

Creating and sustaining a thriving culture won't happen if everyone in the company is wandering around anchorless, going through the motions, hoping you've got it right yet not really sure you're connected to anything more than the company IP address.

Getting to your core purpose statement, individually or as a company, can take quite a bit of mental and emotional to-ing and fro-ing until it feels just right to you. It's much, much more than your profession, your industry, your product or service, your role in life as, say, a parent – even though these will very likely be the avenues by which you keep working towards and living your core purpose.

Once you've got there, it will make sense of and 'inform' every decision you make and action you take.

The equation to define your core purpose is simple:

Core Values + Strengths/Passions = Purpose

- To get clear on your own core purpose, the place to start is your values, which are fundamental beliefs or a moral code – those things that drive your behaviour and are what you stand for. One of the best tools to use, and it's free, is the Values In Action (VIA) Character Strength Survey. You can also use any number of other self-assessment values tools available free on-line.

- Using a tool like Alex Linley's The Strengths Profile, work out what your strengths and passions are – a) what you're good at, b) what energisise you and you love doing c) what you either do a lot or would like to do more of.

- Once you've clarified these key things that make you tick, then think about how they play out in your life, at home and at work.

- Now select your top three to five values, the things that define your life, then do the same with your passions or strengths.

- Using these values, passions and strengths, develop your core purpose statement. Keep it simple, just one or two sentences that nail it at a deep level for you, and make sure it's self-explanatory. You'll know when you've got it, trust me on this, you will know.

Here are a couple of examples of company core purpose statements to get you going, from very successful companies. And notice that they're all very simple and easy to understand.

WALT DISNEY – To make people happy.

BOEING – To push the leading edge of aviation, taking on huge challenges, doing what others cannot do.

MARRIOTT HOTELS – To make people away from home feel they are among friends and really wanted.

Will people make mistakes occasionally? Hell yeah. That's how we all learn, and if your people are not making the odd mistake, well, let's just say it's a bit like when the kids are quiet for too long. You should definitely be concerned because a) they're not learning, b) they're not innovating, c) they're probably scared of what will happen if they do and d) they're probably planning their escape.

Of course, if they're clear on that trusty old anchor called core purpose, then you can rest easy that the mistakes won't be of Titanic proportions.

The Meaning of Meaning

Here's a final thought to ponder, along with the science behind it. When people understand the 'why', the meaning or purpose, then the 'how' will present itself, and in fact becomes easier to figure out and do. Humans are indeed amazing creatures!

The reality is that at work, from time to time, we're going to have to do shitty stuff, stuff that's not our passion or one of our strengths, if we're to achieve the overall company goals or objectives. What if, instead of having people grumbling or moaning when this happens or worse, just metaphorically downing tools as they utter those fateful words, 'It's not my job', they pulled it together and got the job done? Willingly. Hard to believe?

Here's the thing. When people have a clear sense of meaning – the 'why' – they'll do even very tough stuff, stuff they might not like doing, but they will do it and do it well, without grumbling or engaging in what I like to call BMWs (not those fabulous European cars but Bitching, Moaning and Whinging).

Let's dip into a bit of science again to ground this exciting revelation in some all-important evidence.

Leading researchers on this topic[22] found that 'meaningfulness and happiness are positively correlated, so they have much in common … whereas happiness was focused on feeling good in the_present, *meaningfulness integrated past, present and future, and sometimes meant feeling bad'*.

Take a moment to absorb that little gem. What it means is that people will willingly do things that actually lead to them feeling not so happy, as long as it's connected to meaning and purpose, yours and theirs.

So, if you haven't already, the very first thing to do is to set aside time to clarify your core purpose, then work with your team members to clarify theirs (a word of warning, in some instances you might need to handle this confidentially and with care, as this exercise could potentially reveal a poor cultural fit, which might explain a lot – more about that later).

---

22 - *Some Key Differences between a Happy Life and a Meaningful Life*, Baumeister, Vohs, Aaker and Garbinsky, *Journal of Positive Psychology* 2013, Vol. 8, Issue 6

If you're not clear on your company core purpose, then see if you *can* find out and then get your head around it. Because if you're not clear, you can be certain no one else knows either.

And if your company doesn't appear to have a core purpose (believe me, it's not uncommon), well that's another whole discussion.

Chapter 5

THE GIFT OF YOUR ATTENTION

If you want to influence anyone to do anything; if you want people to 'come with you' when you're doing tough stuff or going through change; if you want to reap the rewards, personal and profit wise that come with an engaged workforce; if you want to build a thriving culture – you have to 'earn the right'. And you have to keep on earning it, day in, day out.

For starters, this won't happen when you don't *really* listen to people, when you assume, talk at, or present to people. Or worse, get into the 'uhu … uhu … uhu … ' method of hurrying people up so you can talk.

I regularly get asked to work with people, from new recruits to senior executives, coaches, managers and team leaders, who, from the feedback they receive, seem to have a sort of mental blank when it comes to consistently and regularly listening to people.

While this often seems to come from a 'good place' – keen to demonstrate credibility, knowledge, add value or to get things done quickly – there is a very big difference between *being interested* (what other people, your direct reports or colleagues want us to be in relation to their challenges and needs), and *being interesting* (the let-me-tell-you-what-*I*-think, 'all-singing', all-dancing' presentation talk-fest!).

As Hugh Mackay[23] puts it, one common desire that we all have from time to time, is the desire to be taken seriously. And the way we demonstrate that we're taking someone seriously? By listening.

When was the last time someone really listened to you? I mean *really* listened to you? Especially when you needed them to stop and listen because what you were talking about mattered to you a lot. When did someone listen to you so deeply, and so well, that when you parted ways you thought something along the lines of, 'Finally, someone who really gets me … Wow, they were genuinely interested to hear what I had to say … Seemed to really get what I'm worried about, talking about … Finally someone's taking me seriously on this'.

Ask around and at best you might find some people have lucked on to a great 'professional listener' – maybe someone like a career or life coach, counsellor or psychologist. Or if you're lucky, your partner.

So poor is the state of listening skills around the world, that if you choose, and it is a choice, to really amp up your listening skills, it *will give you* a unique competitive advantage. Which, in an age where people have access to more information than ever, can be the maker or breaker of success in a situation, whether it's building engagement with your direct reports, in a relationship or in a competitive situation with a customer.

And in case you were wondering, people know 100% when you're not listening to them, face-to-face or not.

Now, before you start frowning deeply, and think I've got the wrong end of the stick, give me a few moments to explain (I'd ask you listen but …).

---

23 - *What Makes Us Tick*, Hugh Mackay, Hachette, 2010

Linguists reckon that we spend about 70% to 80% of our waking hours in some form of communication. Carving that up, we spend about 9% writing (including tweeting, texting and on socials), 16% reading, 30% speaking, and **45% listening**. The linguists' studies also confirmed that most of us are pretty poor and inefficient listeners.

So, let's look at a couple of reasons why many of us struggle from time to time with focusing on another person, with really listening to them and letting them know that we are taking them seriously.

Sorry, What Did You Just Say?

Ever had one of those ground-open-up-and-swallow-me moments at school, when you realised all eyes were on you because the teacher had just asked you a question? A question clearly related to what they were just talking about? Maybe it's happened in one of your work meetings – at best embarrassing, at worst a bit of a career-limiting moment right there. Or maybe you've had that sinking feeling of having no idea of where the conversation's at when the other person stops talking? Always a great move for making a good impression on a first date – not.

I think I'm pretty safe then in saying that from time to time, we've probably all practised what's commonly called selective deafness. You know what I mean. You're absorbed in a book, watching your favourite show or football team on TV and there's some background noise along the lines of 'Mum, can you take me to soccer tonight? ... When's dinner? …Honey, can you take the dog for a walk this afternoon?' You hear and respond to the noise with a seemingly appropriate noise of your own, but you're not actually listening.

Why is this? How can we hear and respond but not really listen?

What you might not know is that there are a couple of significant physical challenges we all have, and I do mean all, that can regularly get in the way of really listening.

In our eyes, whatever colour they are, we've got somewhere over 200,000,000 receptors – we don't have to think about seeing, we open our eyes and there it is. In fact, our eyes process so much information that we have some nifty mechanisms in our brains to stop us from blowing a fuse by trying to concentrate on all that information.

Our ears on the other hand only have about 10,000,000 receptors, basically meaning that, first up, we have to work about twenty times harder to listen than we do to see. Why is that you might be askng yourself?

Back to our eat-or-be-eaten past. Protein was the prized food source that determined whether or not our ancestors lived to see another few days. So, no pressure, but when you're about to reel in tonight's family sized happy meal, you don't want anything to distract you. All external noise is blocked out so you can concentrate on bringing home the bacon. Unless, of course, it's a noise that represents danger, and could mean that you're the one on the menu: hence, the 'selective' deafness.

Just to add to this, our wonderful brains can work waaaaaay faster than most people speak – which is about 125 to 150 words per minute. However, we have the mental capacity to understand someone speaking at 400 words per minute (if you think you have trouble now, imagine trying to listen to someone speaking at that speed!).

The difference between speaking and processing speed means that when we give the appearance of listening to the average speaker, we're actually using only about 25% of our mental capacity. We still have 75% to do something else with. (And before you go, 'YIPPEE, more time', don't get me started on the myth of multitasking.)

So, our minds wander. And our brains, kind of like toddlers, get bored easily. That's a lot of 'air time' up there folks and so we fill it with – you guessed it – thoughts about what we're going to say next, what question to ask next, panicking about what they're going to ask us next or just idle internal chat totally unrelated to the conversation: 'I wonder where she got those shoes …Is the coffee shop still open? …I've heard ths all before, I know just what they need' You get the drift, the mental drift away from the conversation.

If you're going to *really* listen to someone then you fundamentally have to make a conscious choice to 'switch on' your listening, keep it switched on and to focus on the other person. Because while most of us are born with the ability to hear, listening is in fact a learned skill.

Hands up, how many of you were taught to listen?

Best estimates in school curricula around the world are that if you're lucky, about 9% of teaching time is spent on this essential life skill. I recall that I was certainly told to shut up a lot, but I don't recall ever being taught to listen.

What this means is that we spend the least amount of time learning what we need to spend the most amount of time doing – listening – if we want to earn the right with people and, in the process, build trust.

In one of my all-time favourite books *The Seven Habits of Highly Effective People*[24], Steven Covey notes that when we feel understood, taken seriously, we feel affirmed and validated. He coined the expression: 'Seek first to understand, and then to be understood', which needs to become a bit of a mantra, reminding you of the need to listen to the other person, to 'earn the right', before you can expect them to listen to or be influenced by you.

---

24 - *The Seven Habits of Highly Effective People*, Steven Covey, Simon & Schuster, 1989

Given how rarely most of us experience really being listened to, it really is then all about giving someone the gift of your attention.

Listen Up!

How do you know if someone's interested in you? And I don't mean through the 'beer goggles' on a Friday night. It's when they ask questions, based on what you've been talking about, broadening their understanding and taking the conversation down a sort of funnel towards a shared understanding and clarity. Sounds easy, huh?

Let's unpack that a bit.

Ever asked someone a question and it seemed like you'd just hit a sort of verbal artery? In some situations, maybe you were wondering how on earth you were going to reply or get the conversation back on track, or maybe it was a case of, 'Well that's an hour of my life I'll never get back … '.

Here's the weird thing: if you want to earn the right to influence anyone, you have to let yourself be influenced first. Mind-bending, hey? And here's the kicker. That means the other person should be doing most of the talking, roughly a 70/30 split between them talking and you talking. 'But wait,' I hear you say, 'didn't we just mention out of control conversations?'

And that's the point: controlling the conversation. That's the part you play as a master listener, so that you'll leave the other person with the clear impression that you were genuinely interested, that you really want to understand them, their story or their concerns.

If you picture a funnel, that'll give you an idea of what a good conversation looks like, one where you're focused on using a critical 'earn the right' skill.

Just how powerful is this kind of listening?

Some years ago, I was running a program with a group of energy technicians who'd been flown in to Sydney from various rural areas for a three-day training program. For many it was their first trip to the 'big smoke' and so some of them took up the company's offer to bring their partners with them.

On day two of the program, we covered listening skills and as they headed off for the evening, I reminded them to try the funneling questioning/listening technique overnight with anyone they met up with or talked to.

The next day, as I was grabbing a coffee before starting, a chap who'd been fairly quiet and reserved up to that point tapped me on the shoulder and said to me, 'I wanted to thank you, this program has been life-changing for me'.

You could have knocked me down with a feather – this is definitely not something I'd ever expected to hear, especially after just two days of a learning and development program! I mean, I think I'm pretty good but …

I asked him if he was okay with telling me how the program had changed his life, and this is what emerged.

After 40 years of marriage, he and his wife who lived in a very small country town, had got to the point where divorce seemed to be the only solution to their marital problems. Being such a small town, there was only one family law lawyer, a friend, and so with the trip to Sydney coming up, he and his wife booked separate rooms and had made appointments with two different divorce lawyers in town for later that week.

After the previous day's session, he said that he'd thought deeply about the problems in his marriage (believe me, I was somewhat uncomfortable too at this point, yet he wanted to keep talking). His wife, who he said he still cared about very deeply, had said that one of the biggest problems for her was that he never listened to her.

When he got back to the hotel, armed with a simple listening tool he'd never seen or tried before, he knocked on her door and suggested they have dinner together. She agreed. They headed out and then didn't leave the restaurant until after 11pm. As they walked back to the hotel, his wife said, 'Do you know, that's the first time in 40 years that I feel like you really listened to me'.

The upshot was that they sat on the hotel room balcony for another couple of hours and talked some more. By the time he headed back to his room, they'd decided to cancel the meetings with the lawyers, and were arranging counselling instead, all because he listened.

LISTENING AND STRENGTHSPOTTING
Earlier, I talked about Alex Linley and his team at CAPPfinity who created the Strengths Profile. Alex Linley[25] also created a sort of 'here's one you can use at work or home' tool as well, what he called the 10 Top Strengthspotting Tips.

The tool is based around Linley and his team's observations that when we get people talking about their strengths, even if they're not aware of them, people give you a lot of clues that you're on to something good. Using your best listening skills, here are the questions you can ask yourself and others:

ALEX LINLEY'S TOP TEN STRENGTHSPOTTING TIPS

1. Childhood memories: What do you remember doing as a child that you still do now – but most likely much better? Strengths often have deep roots from our earlier lives.

2. Energy: What activities give you an energetic buzz when you are doing them? These activities are very likely calling on your strengths.

---

25 - *Average to A+: Realising Strengths in Yourself and Others*, by Alex Linley, published by CAPP Press, 2008

3. Authenticity: When do you feel most like the 'real you'? The chances are that you will be using your strengths in some way.

4. Ease: See what activities come naturally to you and at which you excel – sometimes, it seems, without even trying. These will likely be your strengths.

5. Attention: See where you naturally pay attention. You're more likely to focus on things that are playing to your strengths.

6. Rapid learning: What are the things that you have picked up quickly, learning them almost effortlessly? Rapid learning often indicates an underlying strength.

7. Motivation: What motivates you? When you find activities that you do simply for the love of doing them, they are likely to be working from your strengths.

8. Voice: Monitor your tone of voice. When you notice a shift in passion, energy and engagement, you're probably talking about a strength.

9. Words and phrases: Listen to the words you use. When you're saying 'I love to ... ' or 'It's just great when ... ' the chances are that it's a strength to which you are referring.

10. 'To do' lists: Notice the things that never make it on to your 'to do' list. Things that always seem to get done often reveal an underlying strength that means we never need to be asked to do it!

As a bit of an undercover experiment and as part of my Positive Psychology studies, I decided to do a bit of surreptitious strengths spotting with a couple of strangers – two young lads manning the checkout in my local grocery store on different days. Nothing creepy or weird, no stalking, just a few questions to get them talking about their studies.

From their reactions, one, it turned out, was clearly studying subjects in line with his strengths and passion. As I asked him questions about his degree, he noticeably shifted from bored as he packed my groceries (who wouldn't be bored doing that all day, unless of course it's a strength) to chatty, energised and happy to talk. When I asked him how he was finding the year-end exams, he said, 'They're a breeze when you're doing something you love and you've always wanted to do'. Then I asked him where he'd like to work in the future. As he talked, his face 'lit up' and he used phrases like 'I can't wait … I love the idea of … '.

The next day, I lined up and chatted to another young lad. He was almost finished his degree but he didn't know what he wanted to do. He was quite flat, his voice lacked any energy and he had to think about his answers. He said he was studying what his parents thought would be a good degree for getting a job. I asked him what he thought he'd rather have studied. He said, 'I'm so caught up in this study that I don't really know what I want to do'. He looked quite miserable, clearly didn't really want to talk, his voice was quite low and he looked down a lot.

Not long after, in a coaching skills program I was running, I asked for a volunteer to help me demonstrate what happens when you get people talking about strengths, clearly an important aspect of coaching people. I framed the demonstration by referring to the figures from the study by Linley et al, showing the impact on productivity of managing people's performance with an emphasis on weaknesses (-26.8%) versus an emphasis on strengths (+ 36.4%).

Interestingly, my volunteer said he was determined 'not to give anything away'. Tough crowd. Yet as he answered questions about things he didn't like doing, his weaknesses, he folded his arms and legs tight, struck quite a defensive pose and sunk into his chair. He went quiet, his responses got more and more clipped and he seemed to be being careful of what he was saying. He then laughed nervously and said, 'Can we move on now?'

I've summed up what happened below.

Talking About Weaknesses

- Hesitant speech

- Used negative words and phrases: 'I'm hopeless … I try to avoid it at all costs … Hate it … Do it if I absolutely have to'.

- Had to think about answers

- Body was closed, virtually no gestures

- Looked embarrassed, appeared uneasy and not wanting to engage in the conversation

- Began to avoid eye contact

- Clipped, short answers

- Flat affect

- Looked away frequently

- Got the sense that he was uncomfortable and wanted me to move on – which he then asked me to do!

- Made comments like, 'I don't feel authentic … It really drains me … I'm always on my guard … Worrying I'll stuff up or get caught out'.

Talking About Strengths

- Laughed a lot

- Answers appeared more definite, didn't have to consider his answers

- More confident in manner and responses

- More animated, used his arms in wide, open gestures

- Leaned back, more relaxed posture

- Eye contact, smiled

- More voice modulation

- Used phrases like, 'Love it … Want to do it every day … My brain just seems to work better when I'm doing (the strength-based activity) … Don't have to think about what I'm doing, things just seem to come to me'.

- Spoke for around three times longer about strengths compared to time spent on weaknesses

- Was happy to keep talking, was more of a conversation rather than me having to 'mine' for information

Some key take-outs? Once you start listening and strength spotting, it's easy to notice when people are talking about strengths; it feels good for both people in the conversation, as people are clearly more energised.

In short, if you want an increasingly profitable company, where people are doing what they're best at, the culture thrives, trust is built, employees are engaged, rapport is developed, teams work well together, where you coach people, demonstrate real empathy and deep understanding – all powerful relationship-builders – then you'd better get busy listening.

Chapter 6

WHAT'S THE STORY WITH TELLING STORIES AT WORK?

Want to learn something simple you can do that only takes minutes, could make a big difference in getting your message across and help you to influence and persuade people when you really need to? Start telling good stories.

Basically, we've been telling each other stories ever since there were people to tell stories to. Stories to pass on social mores, to keep people safe from danger, behavioural norms, tall tales and true, cautionary tales, how-tos for all the sorts of situations we humans found ourselves in from time to time through millennia – even passing on recipes from your great greats.

These stories often 'travelled' intact, a very long way through time, sometimes without even being written down. That's amazing when you think about it – and yes, there's a survival-in-the-Savannah reason why our brains are wired to find good stories compelling and easy to remember. Hold that thought …

What our ancestors figured out was that for the new kids in the cave to know how to feed themselves, steer clear of danger and stick together, then that information had to be transmitted in a form that would make an impact and stick, so that they would survive and so would the next generation.

We've talked about meaning and purpose, and how important it is for people to connect and engage with your company. So, I'm sure by now you've got your head around the whole core purpose thing. Because that's a given.

One way for people to get clear on your meaning and purpose is to tell a story or stories that demonstrate what your company's core purpose is, along with stories that paint the picture of what living the company's values looks like. We are in fact 'meaning making' creatures, and what will happen in the absence of a story you've shared about some important aspect of your business – well, people being people they'll fill in the gaps, put their own version of two and two together, pass the event or information (if there is any) through the 'filters' of their own experience and make a decision or come to a conclusion.

Sherlock Holmes most of us are not, so the danger of course is that the decisions people make or the conclusions they arrive at, with the best of intentions, could be a bit on the wrong-end-of-the-stick, wide of the mark or even dodgy side.

Powerpoint or Power Story?

Imagine you're the CEO of one of the world's biggest pharmaceutical companies and you're about to walk in and ask the board to approve a hit on your bottom line of several million non-recoupable dollars. Wearing your best suit fresh from the dry cleaner, shoes squeaky clean, tie straight, you confidently walk into the boardroom, footsteps muffled by the plush carpet, and quietly pop your laptop and papers down on the six-metre long polished oak table. Armed with facts, figures and a fabulously detailed and researched PowerPoint presentation, you set about convincing the board to agree to your multi-million dollar spend.

Or, you walk in empty handed, with not a shred of doubt in your mind that your multi-million dollar decision is right and will be approved. Then you tell them a story about the horrific disease your brilliant research scientists have found a cure for, the millions of people living in abject poverty in Africa who are the most affected by this disease, and remind them of why the company's founding fathers set up the company.

Which do you think would be most effective? And indeed was?

Given the title of this chapter, there's no prizes for guessing it was the story linked to core purpose that clinched the deal in 1991 for then CEO of Merck, P. Roy Vagelos, with no push back from the board, as related in *Built to Last*[26].

From its start in 1935, Merck's core purpose was articulated as, 'Above all, let's remember that our business success means victory against disease and help to humankind'. For years, Merck's scientists, attracted no doubt by working for a company with such a noble core purpose, had been trying to find a cure for a hideous disease that affected over a million people in developing countries. (WARNING! If you're squeamish about gross medical stuff, skip ahead to the next paragraph.) River blindness is caused by parasites that get into body tissue, ending up in the eyes, causing very painful blindness. And you thought that ingrown toenail was bad …

A cure, Mectizan, was finally found by the Merck researchers, so the Merck team swung into production, along with sorting out arrangements for transportation and distribution. The financial 'catch' was, however, that the millions of people most affected by this hideous disease lived in developing countries and couldn't pay for it. Nonetheless, plans for distribution went ahead, while requests were made to various government agencies for

---

26 - *Built to Last: Habits of Visionary Companies* Jim Collins and Jerry Porras, William Collins, 1994

financial help. Nothing doing. So, Mr Vagelos found himself in a very difficult position; indeed a very difficult, multi-million dollar position.

As he sat, no doubt like many a CEO making a difficult decision, alone and pondering what to do, our man at the top had a moment of absolute clarity that turned the decision from difficult to, well, easy.

The board agreed with his decision and the drug was supplied, at no cost, to the poor souls suffering from this terrible disease.

When asked how he made the decision, Vagelos described it as what we might call today a 'no-brainer' once he reflected on Merck's core purpose, 'Victory against disease and help to humankind'. If the company hadn't supplied the drug, people such as the research scientists, who'd slaved away for years over a Bunsen burner to find the cure, would very likely have become disenchanted and demoralised, and possibly even leave Merck. Whilst acknowledging the short-term cost, he went on to say that he could only begin to imagine the long-term cost to Merck from the knock-on effect of such a disconnect from core purpose, an effect which would no doubt have travelled to other parts of the company too.

What I just did there (I'm sure you picked it up!) was share a story demonstrating how storytelling can work at work. Mind-bending, huh? This is an example of a great story that I use when I want to help anyone understand the power of having a living, breathing core purpose, company or personal, how that translates into behaviour and can help make even the toughest decisions that much easier.

Change Your Story, Change Your Culture

If you've been involved in any major company change initiatives, or studied change management, you've no doubt come across John Kotter of Harvard Business School. He's something of a change management guru and has studied and worked with some of the world's largest and most complex organisations, as they go through the unholy mess that is all too often part and parcel of most major changes. He made the following, very astute observations about how to get people on board with change.[27]

'The central issue is never strategy, structure, culture, or systems. The core of the matter is always about changing the behaviour of people. Behaviour change happens mostly by speaking to people's feelings,' he says. 'This is true even in organisations that are very focused on analysis and quantitative measurement, even among people who think of themselves as smart in an MBA sense. In highly successful change efforts, people find ways to help others see the problems or solutions in ways that influence emotions, not just thought.'

Kotter makes a great point and yet, all too often, organisations are overly focused on the technical, quantitative, analytical, operational and project management aspects of change (or in fact of the day-to-day running of the business). And this is at the expense of the adaptive, qualitative aspects of building a thriving company; you know, all those so-called 'touchy-feely' things I've been talking about that we now know are what leads to engagement, which in turn leads to increased wellbeing and profit.

Ever tried to argue your point of view with someone who sees things differently? Maybe thrown in a few well-placed facts (real, not fake or alternative) and figures? What tends to happen? Typically, you and your sparring partner will dig in your respective heels, umbrage may well be taken, and you either agree to disagree or worse, amygdalae fly off and, well, you know the rest …

A well-placed and appropriate story can be the thing that causes people to have those wonderful 'A-ha! Now I get it'

---

27 - *Change or Die*, Alan Deutschman, HarperBusiness, 2007

moments. They can also move people to take the action you want them to take, break down barriers and turn something complex into something relatable and far simpler for people to grasp. Stories connect to our wonderful imaginations and can make things far more meaningful, relevant and real in a way that cold, hard facts can't. Make no mistake – stories can be very, very powerful and valuable tools, especially when it comes to your culture.

Stories can change the way we think, how we act and feel, and guide our decisions especially in ambiguous situations. A good story or two can influence and motivate people to achieve what they might have thought was too hard or even impossible. Gandhi, for example, changed the history of a nation through stories, not guns.

In short, using sometimes just a few words, stories can capture the culture of an organisation, show people how to live in a way aligned with your values and help build trust in teams.

That's a lot of impact from the simple act of sharing a good story.

So, stay tuned as we dip into the art (and science) of storytelling, what you can do to engage peoples' hearts and minds and positively impact your culture even when you're sharing difficult or controversial information with a potentially hostile, resistant or dubious audience.

And yes, we'll get into a bit more neuroscience for non-neuroscientists, so you can get a handle on why stories, if they're not already, need to become part of your thriving-culture tool-box.

Your Brain on Storytelling

Strap yourselves in for a moment while I delve into one of my favourite places – that amazing neck-top computer sitting on top of your shoulders.

Picture your brain for a second. Now, imagine this: when we hear just facts and figures, fMRIs show that only a couple of places in our brains light up – those to do with listening and word processing. That's pretty much it. Not much action in terms of hormones either, those little gems that can do so much fabulous stuff for our minds and bodies.

What changes, when we're given information in the form of an engaging and well-told story, is that anywhere up to seven areas of the brain light up, especially if that story involves a lot of sensory information, appealing to our five senses of smell, sight, sound, taste and feeling. In the hands of a master story-teller, what happens in the brain are the same reactions as if we were experiencing the situation ourselves – empathy, real empathy.

Paul Zak and fellow neuroscientist William Casebeer (great surname!) found some other important and interesting things happen in our brains when we get told or shown these kinds of stories. Oxytocin, yep, the 'tend and befriend' hormone, is released and creates feelings of empathy, relatedness and closeness. We also get a hit of dopamine, the neurotransmitter connected to motivation, reward and addiction, when we listen to a story with an emotional connection.

Think about the ads we see every day. Think the so-called Mad Men might know a thing or two about the power of a good story to persuade us to change our ways, or part with our hard-earned cash?

Now you can see why it was so important for our ancestors to be great storytellers, if the 'cave gang' was to stay together and survive.

A Few Storytelling Tips

- To get the most out of your story, you need to be clear on your action objective (what you want people to do as a result of what you're about to tell them), as well as your emotional objective (how you want them to feel and behave).

- **Action Objective** – What's my outcome? Your action objective needs to be a clear action stating what you *do* want people to do, not what you don't want. Examples – endorse, change, support, accept, use, implement, lead the process, get involved.

- **Emotional Objective** – How do I want them to feel and behave after hearing this information? Examples – excited, respected, understood, motivated, inspired, **calm, reassured.**

- **Start collecting and jotting down your stories now.** They don't have to be over the top, outrageous, breathtaking, incredible stories. As you can see, I've peppered this book with stories, many of them popping into my head as I'm typing or thinking about a topic. Just write them down somewhere, brief points, so you can recall and then dip into them when you need to.

- **You can also use other people's stories** – Just acknowledge that it's not yours. *Never* ever try to pass someone else's story off as your own experience. It won't work; trust me on that.

As Paul Zak[28] puts it, 'Character driven stories with emotional content result in a better understanding of the key points a speaker wishes to make and enable better recall of these points … Start off with a compelling human-scale story if you want to boost empathy, cooperation and motivation'.

---

28 - *The Neuroscience of Trust*, Paul J. Zak, Harvard Business Review, January/February 2017

ACHIEVE

- **WANNA KICK MORE GOALS? (HINT: FOCUS ON PEOPLE AND PURPOSE; PROFITS WILL FOLLOW)**

- **HANG ON TO YOUR KNIFE AND FORK – OPTIMISM, PLAY AND OPTIMAL OUTPUT**

Chapter 7

WANNA KICK MORE GOALS?
(Focus on people and purpose; profits will follow)

Many years ago, when I made the move from social worker into my first corporate job, I had trouble understanding the relentlessly cynical, overtly negative, seasoned veterans I worked with, who said things to me like, 'You'll learn … You'll get over yourself soon … You'll see … '.

Baffled but undaunted, along with being blissfully ignorant of what wasn't possible, off I drove in the company provided Toyota Camry into the wide world of sales, a ten-centimetre thick computer printout of client details by my side and the mandatory audio tapes of American sales gurus to keep me pepped up along the way.

To say I didn't know what I was doing was an understatement. Yet despite that, and much to the enormous frustration of the naysayers, I was so darned enthusiastic and excited to be offered what I saw as such a great opportunity that I practically brought in business out of sheer force of personality. The clients loved me and loved what I was doing to help their businesses, I won sales awards left, right and centre, saw monthly bonuses drop in with my salary and put the teeth grinding in the weekly sales meetings down to a cluster of overbites.

Then somewhere around April, I noticed that an even darker pall had descended upon my relentlessly cynical colleagues. The 'You'll sees' were trotted out again as we drove off in a convoy of Camrys to an out of town seaside motel for a sales conference with the boss – the chief cynic, or the CC as I later came to call him. I was about to be inducted into the age-old process of sales forecasting.

It was like a mini Hunger Games, with me a bewildered participant, and went something like this.

Last financial years' and year-to-date sales figures were produced, pored over and dissected. Sales territories and prized clients were fought over, won and lost; there was much gnashing of teeth, some shouting and, in the evening, lots of alcohol consumption. Individual SWOT analyses were done and then shot down in flames by the CC. Expenses, always topical amongst salespeople of course, were thrashed out and easily the cause of the most emotional of outbursts on the part of my veteran colleagues.

After three days of blood, sweat and in some cases tears, we all handed over our sales forecasts to the boss, in my case feeling confident in the knowledge that I'd creamed this year's targets so the increases I'd added I felt sure were more than doable.

And about six weeks later, back came the final locked-in sales targets from the big kahunas, bearing, of course (note the cynicism …) absolutely no resemblance to anything we'd sent off, in my case with sales targets more than double what I'd forecast, and one of the requiring-resuscitation clients I'd rekindled handed over to one of the veterans. Talk about burst your bubble. I did indeed now see …

The CC's explanation? I was earning too much. Translation: you've been too successful so we need to make it harder for you to succeed. Way to go, buddy!

And in case you're wondering, I only hung about for as long as it took for me to be able to add a decent amount of 'time served' to my CV, then moved on swiftly. You've possibly figured out by now that I've got a low tolerance level for people being treated like that, which of course is why I wrote *Culture 101*.

Science tells us that the quickest way to demotivate people and to make sure they don't achieve their goals or targets is to constantly threaten negative consequences (it's why those folks with the heart surgery didn't follow through; threat of imminent death doesn't motivate people, just makes them scared on top of being unwell). Other things that demoralise people and chip away at motivation include conducting surveillance (it's not uncommon to hear that people's emails and work phones are being monitored), constantly negatively evaluating performance and setting unrealistic targets or deadlines. Anything sounding familiar here?

Not sure if we actually needed science to tell us, according to the myriad of culture and engagement surveys, what we already know we don't like. But, it is reassuring to know that when this sort of insane culture and joy-killing micromanagement happens, you're not alone, you are (most likely) right and no, you're not, as I sometimes ended up thinking, completely unreasonable or crazy.

So, we've had a look at what doesn't work and quite possibly had a less-than-ideal experience or two as well, either as a leader trying to hit targets, or as a team member. Now, let's have a look at what is far more likely to work, to help you achieve yours, the company's and your team members' goals.

Goals, Purpose and Kpis

As a leader, getting the balance right between earning the right and achieving can be a bit tricky to say the least. The conundrum is this: you've no doubt got the leadership gig because you're good at what you do, you've achieved results in whatever is your field of expertise, and yet the thing is that you can continue to be productive and still <u>not</u> be a leader – all because you've dropped the earn-the-right ball.

Because now it's not just about your results, but also about the team results, and ultimately the buck does stop with you. So, let's look at a few simple things you can do to get the ball to success rolling (not dropping) for you and your team, and alleviate some of the stress of the balancing act that leadership can indeed be.

Funny. Most people know intuitively that personal, life and work goals are important for a whole raft of reasons. Yet it'd be fair to say that many of us start out with good intentions, but seem to miss the mark, sometimes repeatedly, with achieving a variety of goals. And while the old S.M.A.R.T goals mnemonic is fine, our brains need a bit more convincing when it comes to actually achieving goals.

' … Making lists of short and long terms goals are important for our wellbeing and even daily survival … People make lists for many reasons, however, research has shown that goals are important for several reasons. First, goals give us a sense of purpose, a reason for being. We would be lost without goals. It is also the actual progression towards those goals and not necessarily the attainment of the goal that creates wellbeing (the journey not the destination) … Goals add structure and meaning to our daily life, helping us learn how to manage our time. Thus, as we go through our day and meet smaller sub-goals, our self-esteem and self-efficacy is enhanced … people with aspirations and dreams that are in progress or achievable and **personally meaningful**, are happier than those who do not have them.'[29]

The highlighting is mine – and here's why.

---

29 - *Positive Psychology: Theory, Research and Applications*, Kate Hefferon and Ilona Boniwell, McGraw Hill, 2011

Your first job as a leader, as you negotiate how to balance earning the right with achievement and if you want your life to be that much easier, is to get to know your people well. Not through resumes or all those psych assessments, not in meetings, not talking at them, not by not listening and, quite possibly, not through taking on board the points of view of, for example, your predecessor.

What you do need to do is to meet with your team one-on-one, use your best listening skills and find out their 'why', that all important meaning and purpose I talked about in Chapter 4. And either use something like the Strengths Profile, do some solid strength spotting using Linley's questions, or just straight out ask each person something like, 'If money and time were no object, what would you do for work?' then listen to get some clues about strengths, too.

Even if you've been in the gig for a while now, if anyone in your team is regularly missing goals, it's time to hold up the mirror and ask yourself a question. Because as I've said, the buck does indeed stop with you.

The question? 'Is this an information issue or a motivation issue?'

Hand on heart, can you say you've given this person all the information, resources and appropriate level of support they need to do what's required of them? If the answer's a resounding yes, then you've got a motivation issue on your hands. Personal problems aside, at its most basic, this person is in some way not connected to the job at hand, the goals or targets. And you can bet your frequent flyer points it's got a lot to do with a disconnect from their dreams, their strengths, their goals and what's important to them.

In one of my leadership gigs, I was, against my better judgement, tasked from day one with overseeing the shift to a highly regimented KPI collection procedure, a monitoring process that ticked every single 'what not to do if you want people to thrive and profits grow' box. The company I'd joined had been acquired twelve months before by a bigger fish, and then promptly began to tank. The worse things got, the more the screws got tightened, the closer the scrutiny. Clearly, they'd read and rigidly adhered to some modern-day version of the Dickensian motivation method.

Seasoned employees, with all their knowledge and contacts, left in droves disgusted with the way they were being treated, and this included a couple of my state manager predecessors.

In a short period of time, and to my eternal horror, I became known as The KPI Queen, as I attempted to fulfill the demands of the new owners, whose attitude was very much 'our way or the highway'. Now, I've got no argument with the need to collect various numbers to run a business. But, demanding that people complete KPI forms and submit them hourly? Out of control, utterly demoralising and the biggest buzz kill of all, especially for a sales team. Don't know about you, but like most people I talk to, I have no desire to become known for perpetuating the seagull (or in one over the top case – pterodactyl) style of leadership: swoops, shits and leaves.

You didn't have to be Sigmund Freud to figure out that people were not happy, not at all, and the unhappier they were, the harder of course it got to achieve goals.

Something had to change, and quickly, if I was going to help turn things around, and given the KPI regime was here to stay, I did what I knew best – focused on the people. What I decided to do was to take the team aside and create some personal internal meaning behind what they had to do every day. Remember, as I said earlier, people are not coming to work to help you or the board realise your dreams. They come to work to earn money so they can realise their own dreams, whatever they are.

So, armed with piles of magazines, scissors, glue and a few manila folders, I ran a team session where each person got clear on their own goals and then created a vision board. Then, we worked out what they needed to do to achieve it, down to daily KPI activity, using some good old backwards planning.

The shift in energy was palpable. From then on, any time people found themselves feeling deflated they looked up at their vision board, at their own dreams and pressed on, having grounded the 'daily KPI grind' into something meaningful and relevant to each of them.

Sadly, my efforts at humanising the environment weren't fully appreciated by the powers that were, in particular clashing with the policy of minimal personal items of any kind in desk areas (think back to that zoo habitat folks, think back …). Yet the feedback from the team led me to think, and the results showed, that I was possibly on to something.

Turning Goals into a Vision Board

Most people will gain more, build better understanding and long-lasting mental impact from information by taking it in visually with a lot of colour and images thrown in for good measure.

Remember back to storytelling, and the difference in terms of how much of our brains get involved when we just see or hear facts and figures as opposed to a story? A vision board has the same sort of impact, telling the imagined and desired future story of the person who created it. And given the brain impact, it possibly explains why just writing down your goals (usually to then be put in a drawer or folder somewhere) has far less impact than using a vision board or storyboarding technique.

Simply put, a vision board is a physical representation of your desired future state or reality. It becomes a clear, tangible, sharp image that has meaning and relevance to whoever created it, and which can then keep you focused on achieving your goal. By keeping your goals in front of you and front of mind in this way, you're more likely to become aware of and tuned in to any opportunities, people, information or resources that might help you to take incremental (or bigger!) steps towards achieving your goals, as opposed to if they were written down and placed in a folder somewhere!

The funny thing is, that when you stop faffing about and fully commit to a goal or two, some interesting things start to happen.

> Until one is committed there is hesitancy, the chance to draw back, always ineffectiveness. Concerning all acts of initiative (and creation) there is one elementary truth, the ignorance of which kills countless ideas and splendid plans: that the moment one definitely commits oneself, then Providence moves too. All sorts of things occur to help one that would never otherwise have occurred. A whole stream of events issues from the decision, raising in one's favour all manner of unforeseen incidents and meetings and material assistance, which no man could have dreamed would have come his way. I have learned a deep respect for one of Goethe's couplets: What ever you can do, or dream you can, begin it. Boldness has genius, power and magic in it.

W.H. Murray,
The Scottish Himalayan Expedition

So, where do you begin? You can make a vision board by drawing or painting, or by making a collage using pictures and words cut out of magazines, cards, photographs, old books and so on. A work of art is not what you're looking for here by the way, just whatever works for you. You'll need a couple of selfies printed out too, as you'll need to put yourself into the pictures, having achieved your goal or dream.

Some Points for Vision Boarding

1. Use a manila folder. This is just a good size for carrying with you, sticking above your desk, in a plastic cover in the shower (it's been done!) and takes less time to complete. You can of course go bigger and take a photo to use as your screen saver.

2. Write down your goals for no more than five key areas of your life, e.g. finance, health, family, career and travel. This is just at a high level, what you *do* want. The goals need to be:

- Internally motivated – You're doing it for the sake of doing it, not for money, promotion or fame

- In alignment with your values (use the free VIA assessment online to help clarify your values)

- Something you want to move <u>towards</u>, not because you want to avoid something

- Linked to your life as a whole – complements your other life and work goals

- Flexible – can be tweaked as your situation changes

- Aligned to your strengths but pushes you out of your comfort zone

1. Write the dream or goal in its ideal, completed form, like you're already there. Think about things like what you'll see, smell, feel, taste and who'll be there with you. You don't need to know how it's going to come about. Trust your brain: work out the WHY, keep focused on it and the HOW will pop up eventually. *

2. Divide your manila folder up into different areas for a single goal or area of your life. This means you can include all the important elements for each without it getting too cluttered or complicated. It also helps your mind to focus on it more clearly and easily than if you throw it all in together.

3. Be sure to put yourself in the picture. Show yourself being, doing or having your dream or goal – travelling around the world, holding the letter of offer for your dream job, wearing new clothes, with the keys to your new house, etc.

4. Use lots of colour in your vision board – colour stimulates your brain, too.

5. Show yourself in a setting that's believable for you.

6. Type up and glue your goal statements on the relevant area of your vision board. *'Here I am in the plane on my way to New York, sipping champagne, sitting next to my partner. I'm so excited, and have plenty of money to enjoy this trip.'*

7. Now, all you need to do is to spend a few minutes each day quietly looking at it, thinking yourself into it and giving it some thought. Your brain will start to get busy working on the how.

Now, this whole vision board thing might sound a bit bonkers to some of you, a bit woo-woo even. Yet given what

I've been talking about and how the brain works, have a think about that for a moment – you might just want to give it a try.

You've got nothing to lose. Oh, except those goals for you and your team.

(*It's to do with yet another smart 'app' in your brain. Ever bought a car and suddenly noticed how many others of the same make are around? Heard a new word and now you notice it everywhere? Got pregnant and notice how many other people are too? Interesting, huh?

In the base of your brain, you've got another bouncer of sorts, the reticular activating system (RAS), serving a somewhat different purpose to your amygdalae bouncers. Fact is, at any moment, our brains are exposed to so much information that if we tried to focus on everything, well, we'd blow a fuse or two.

Your RAS has several ways of classifying information into large chunky folders, thereby allowing our brains to focus on what's important. So, when you start to focus on something, like your vision board, things that the RAS would've previously sent off to long-term storage are now sent to front of house. Hence how the *HOW* will start to get clearer, all because you'll start to notice things you very likely wouldn't have before. Have I told you how much I love how we can lelverage all that neuroscience research?)

Team Building – Minus the Paintball

Just a few words about teams and team goals before I move on.

Ask anyone what it's like being part of a team that really hummed or still hums – whether it was a work team, your family, a sports team or a community group – and some surprisingly similar comments emerge: 'We've got each other's backs … Loyal to the team … We trust each other

… All valued for our unique contribution and qualities … Lots of lively debate to nut out problems … Never fearful of voicing a different point of view … No primadonnas … All pitch in when we're up against it'.

Likewise, most of us have probably had the not-so-great experience of being part of a lousy, dysfunctional team – a team full of politics, where unbridled primadonna behaviour and often bullying (both subtle and not so subtle) is rife; goals and targets get missed; difficult issues aren't aired (or if they are, not everyone weighs in, inevitably leading to the 'meeting after the meeting'); and where it feels more like a collection of individuals rather than a committed and focused team – not exactly the formula for a thriving team that's likely to achieve goals, let alone go over and above.

Sound familiar?

While they have their place, sometimes a game of paintball, a few rounds of golf or drinks on a Friday after work, just aren't enough on their own to 'cure what ails' a group of people that just don't seem to be operating as a high performing team.

Here are some tips for a thriving team:

- Recruit for individual strengths, and for what I call the untrainables. Anyone connected to your company core purpose will make it their business to learn about products and procedures.

- Do some team sessions, around team purpose and around vision-boarding.

- Run a get-to-know-and-appreciate-each-other team session with someone qualified to do so, using the Strengths Profile, or even DiSC or the Myers Briggs Type Indicator.

- Get to know people one-on-one and find out what drives them.

- Build trust individually and with the team as a whole.

- Tell the team stories to demonstrate who you are, what your values are and how things work around here.

- Get the team to agree on a set of guidelines on how you'll all behave in meetings so everyone feels safe to speak up, even on contentious issues. This isn't what I call 'meetings 101' but is about things like no raised voices, no swearing, no judgement, one person to speak at a time, etc. You know, basic good manners.

A couple of leading researchers in the field of motivation and goal achievement, Deci and Ryan[30] summed it up this way: 'Our three basic needs (are) autonomy, relatedness and competence. When intrinsically motivated, people *want* to engage in the activity; they need no external prompts, promises or threats to initiate action. Being intrinsically motivated also enhances wellbeing, engagement and success'.

Implement just one of the ideas here to start with and you're on your way to achieving your goals, helping your team achieve their personal and work goals and to leaving a legacy of success when you move on.

---

30 - *Self-Determination Theory and the Facilitation of Intrinsic Motivation, Social Development and Wellbeing*, R. Ryan and E. Deci, American Psychologist Vol 55: 68 -78

Chapter 8

HANG ON TO YOUR KNIFE AND FORK – optimism, play and optimal output

For those of you old enough to remember, the early 1990s was when Australia had 'the recession we had to have', according to the then Federal Treasurer, Paul Keating.

And what a recession it was.

When people talk about the more recent global financial crisis (GFC), I'm always reminded of that famous scene from *Crocodile Dundee* when a would-be thief confronts him and his date with a six-inch knife. Pulling out his *huge* Bowie knife, Dundee says, 'That's not a knife, this is a knife'. The early '90s recession, the one we 'had to have', was the Australian economy equivalent of that Bowie knife.

Sobering times indeed. Every day we heard about more businesses going to the wall, head-shaking-in-disbelief bankruptcies amongst the previously rich and famous, people living in houses with negative equity as property prices tanked and mortgage interest rates hit 19%, overseas investment evaporating, with all this leading to unemployment reaching an all-time double digit high.

Not being one to shy away from a challenge, my next foray into corporate life was, naturally, a move into what was then one of the top recruitment companies in Australia. Friends and family who didn't think I was barking mad ('You're joining an employment agency during the worst unemployment we've ever had?') considered me very brave. Me? I had a different point of view.

Not only was I thrilled to be selected to join a top-notch company out of a field of some 150 applicants (no doubt many desperate for a job) but I also figured that if I could make it in this kind of job during the toughest of times, well the good times would be a breeze. Like I said, I like a challenge.

As you can imagine, with so few jobs on offer, recruiting companies all over the country were in a serious competition for their livelihood. Fee discounting was the strategy du jour with clients driving the price down, leading to recruitment companies barely making ends meet and consequently many having to lay off their own staff. Of course, many such companies didn't survive.

We, however, were tasked with a different strategy, a strategy that even today I consider not only ballsy, but also downright smart and a perfect demonstration of what realistic optimism is all about.

Not long into my new job, the directors called the whole company into a meeting. As you can imagine, fear was running high, amygdalae bouncers were flexing muscle and faces were pretty grim as we sat down in the training room, many expecting to hear the worst – layoffs.

What the directors said to us was gold, pure solid gold. First up, reassuring words along the lines of 'we've got a great team here and we have no intention of losing a single one of you great people'. (Whew, a collective breath out …)

The strategy we were tasked with implementing? For starters, no discounting. Discounting they said, and I agree, not only cheapens your brand in people's minds, but have you ever tried to get your price back up once you've offered a hefty discount? Good luck, as they say, with that – because for starters, it's going to take you a long, long time.

Discounting also starts to make you appear desperate for business and therefore potentially risky to do business with. Hold steady, our directors said, in your teams work out some value-add things you can offer clients to throw into the mix, like psych testing. Short-term cost for sure, but way less than the cost of that long road back to pre-discount fee levels, with of course the across the board loss of income in the meantime.

Slightly unbelieving, with many people a bit nervous and admitting they thought no one would want to pay top dollar when everyone was discounting, off we went. We were however, very reassured by the directors' realistic optimism and their genuine faith in us. And it worked. For all the reasons they'd said. Blue chip organisations came to us in droves, nervous about dealing with the discounters, the company flourished through the worst of the recession and not only did no one lose their job, we were putting people on to cope with the torrent of work.

Realistic Optimism

Optimism. Look it up. Because interestingly, apart from meaning a tendency to look on the more favourable side of events and to expect the most favourable outcome, the root of the word is from the Latin word for the greatest good of mankind. Whoa, impressive!

What optimism isn't about is some unrealistic, frivolous, devil-may-care, off with the pixies way of looking at the world. In terms of *Culture 101*, and in the context of positive leadership, it's about a number of things, individual, team and company-wide. Even, no *especially*, when things seem to be stacked against you, the outlook is a bit grim and the seduction of a fault-finding, witch-hunting, finger-pointing, full-blown pessimist's-paradise exercise could be quite strong.

Seeing things through the pessimist's grimy lens is all about the status quo and in the long term, history shows us, will very likely lead to a gradual slide into irrelevancy (ouch!), being a target for a hostile takeover, or worse, shutting the doors altogether.

Realistic optimism, on the other hand, is about garnering what resources you have, learning what you can from things that went pear-shaped or from unexpected events, letting bygones be bygones and taking a sort of a 'here's what we've got, here's where we're going … what if … ' future-focused view of the world.

It's also about 'hanging on to your knife and fork', because as we know, that means there are more goodies coming.

Reckon Shackleton was a realist? Reckon he was in no doubt that the odds were stacked against him and his crew? Reckon, given his knowledge of Antarctica from previous trips, he might have had good reason to expect he could find help? In case you haven't worked it out, the story still blows me away.

Realistic optimism is also undoubtedly what allowed many companies to thrive during the Great Depression. History shows that those companies that were open to being innovative, and who kept a positive focus on the future, did far better compared to those who discounted, cut costs and jobs, hunkered down and waited until it all 'blew over'.

Most of the successful ones also focused on one primary thing: emotional connection with people. They kept themselves visible to their consumers, to the general community and to their people, knowing that to appear to 'abandon' people at that time would be disastrous for their future brand and positioning. And they were right, with many of their competitors disappearing altogether.

Think back to Chapter 3 when I talked about the four leadership traits that come up in survey after survey – trust, compassion, stability and hope. An organisation that fosters a realistically optimistic view of the world you operate in is one that connects to that number one leadership trait – *trust*. It demonstrates *compassion* – an 'I get that things don't look so great right now, you might be worried or scared' kind of compassion. It also connects to the need for *hope* about the future and, if history tells us anything, it's that this kind of realistic optimism also leads to *stability*.

So, how can you get your people focused on an optimistic view of the world when things seem to have to gone to hell in a hand-basket, and keep them and your culture thriving?

Some Tips for Shifting to a Realistic Optimistic Perspective

1. Reframing is a simple technique where you get people to consider an event from different perspectives, rather than looking at it through one lens, one that might not be serving them or the situation very well. It might be as simple as considering how someone else would see this problem – say, a child, a doctor or your clients.

2. It also helps to ask what else could be happening? What's another explanation? What else could be going on? These sorts of questions can help shift focus from a pessimistic, catastrophic, everything-looks-bad frame of mind, to something far more realistic and potentially useful.

3. Martin Seligman[31], quite possibly one of the best-known researchers and writers on the topic of optimism, talks about reframing events through three different lenses. This simple checklist has saved my sanity many times, even on the toughest of days. Along a scale of one to ten:

- How PERMANENT is this? Will it last forever or eventually diminish or pass?

- How PERSONAL is it? Is it really all about me?

- How PERVASIVE is it? Does this affect all areas of my life?

4. You can also use another simple, two question reality check when dealing with tough stuff:

- Do I/we have any control over this at all? No? Then stop the BMWing and move on to the next question.

- What **do I/we have** direct or indirect control over?

A word of warning, there will no doubt be difficult times – loss of a big deal, mass redundancies, dealing with the client from hell – and many people will need time to talk about and process what's happened.

Once people have had an appropriate amount of time and support to get stuff off their chest, this is about dusting yourselves off, picking yourselves up and focusing on the way forward.

And the great thing is that as you build a positive, strengths-based culture on a bedrock of trust, meaning and purpose, science tells us that people will bounce back far more quickly.

---

31 - *Learned Optimism: How to Change Your Mind and Change Your Life*, Martin E.P. Seligman, Random House, 1991

Play at Work

Who else to start off a section on the importance of playfulness and light heartedness at work than the great John Cleese:

'I think we all know that laughter brings relaxation, and that humour makes us playful, yet how many times have important discussions been held where really original and creative ideas were desperately needed to solve important problems, but where humour was taboo because the subject being discussed was {air quotes} "so serious"?

'This attitude seems to me to stem from a very basic misunderstanding of the difference between "serious" and "solemn".

'Now I suggest to you that a group of us could be sitting around after dinner, discussing matters that were extremely serious like the education of our children, or our marriages, or the meaning of life (and I'm not talking about the film), and we could be laughing, and that would not make what we were discussing one bit less serious.

'Solemnity, on the other hand … I don't know what it's for. I mean, what is the point of it? The two most beautiful memorial services that I've ever attended both had a lot of humour, and it somehow freed us all, and made the services inspiring and cathartic.

'But solemnity? It serves pomposity, and the self-important always know with some level of their consciousness that their egotism is going to be punctured by humour — that's why they see it as a threat. And so they dishonestly pretend that their deficiency makes their views more substantial, when it only makes them feel bigger.

'No, humour is an essential part of spontaneity, an essential part of playfulness, an essential part of the creativity that we need to solve problems, no matter how "serious" they may be.'

Like many of you reading this, possibly at an airport somewhere, I fly a lot for work, around Australia and overseas. As frequent flyers know and are eternally grateful for, security and safety is paramount and is understandably taken very seriously. Like John Cleese though, it's the solemnity (and at times downright aggression) I don't get.

Like I said, I get that it's serious and I am so very glad it is. I don't get why it has to be so darn solemn and downright unfriendly.

On a recent trip through Sydney International Airport, I was in the queue, snaking my way to immigration. I was behind a gorgeous loved-up young couple, very excited and, from what I could overhear, on their honeymoon. Blow me down if Cruella De Ville's long lost Australian cousin didn't come over, practically pole-vaulted over the ropes and yelled (and I mean top-of-lungs-in-case-anyone-in-Melbourne-didn't-hear yelled) at them to stop holding hands and stand behind one another. Another couple of bubbles of joy sadly burst, as we all put our heads down and got on with the business of running the gauntlet.

How the security and safety message seems to translate, especially when you're travelling internationally, is that once you step through that door to the immigration area, you're basically on your own. No rights apparently, no questions, no answers given, heads down, don't attract attention to yourself, don't text, don't call, don't laugh, don't look too happy, don't talk. Just get through the scrutiny of immigration, don't engage, grin (metaphorically, mind you, don't want to draw attention to yourself remember) and bear the various indignities of the security hurdles. By the time you pop out the other side, it's sometimes feels like you've just been acquitted.

(I for one am never so happy as when I encounter that first perfume spruiker on the 'other side', and still get nostalgic when I get whiff of Chanel No. 5.)

John Cleese makes it clear – there's serious and then there's solemn.

And that no man's land between the farewell tears, selfies, promises of Instagram posts and the relief of making it through to duty-free, well, it's solemn in the extreme. Everyone it seems is a suspect and is guilty until proven innocent, when we've made it through the final security hurdle.

The thing is it is entirely possible to be serious about something at work and actually have a bit of harmless fun. I used to work in Accident and Emergency and the Intensive Care Unit (or Expensive Scare Unit as we called it) at a major hospital, so I know it's possible and in fact absolutely necessary if you're going to stay sane and healthy.

Case in point: in 2014, to coincide with the final instalment of the Hobbit trilogy, Air New Zealand in a world first created a safety procedures video that became known as the Most Epic Safety Video Ever. And though the stuffed shirts at the Civil Aviation Authority (I know, and I am eternally grateful that they do indeed have our safety uppermost in mind) tried hard to shoot it down, it passed all the tests for getting the safety message across.

Being a seasoned traveller, like a lot of the other seasoned travellers, I'm usually head down in a book or my kindle prior to take off, and usually give scant regard to the safety demonstration (apologies to any flight crew reading this, it's not about you, it's what you've been given to work with). But, on a trip to New Zealand in 2014, I actually watched the safety video twice!

As you now know a lot about how our brains work perhaps you can see why such a different, creative, colourful safety video had the desired effect on passengers, even jaded frequent flyers like me. Different – tick, creative – tick and colourful – tick – three things that wake up our brain, stop the RAS reaction of 'Oh, it's just another one of those safety videos, nothing to see here folks, off to storage', and cause us to pay attention. And they keep 'em coming with new creative safety demo videos every few months – another tick. Way to go, Air New Zealand!

Not surprisingly, many other airlines have followed suit and, like Air New Zealand, have learnt that if you want to keep people tuned in to an important message you need to change it up and have a bit of fun.

And yes, you guessed it, when we have a bit of fun, when we laugh, more of those wellbeing-enhancing, amazing hormones get released. Here's just a few of the free, absolutely no-cost, resilience-building, stress-reducing, immunity-boosting side effects of having a laugh, of being a bit lighthearted and playful at work:

- A cocktail of fabulous hormones is released including endorphins, serotonin and growth hormone all of which boost your immune system (told you this was about more than that annual flu shot)

- Stimulates circulation and helps relax your muscles

- Decreases the secretion of cortisol and adrenaline – a counter to those shocking stats about Monday morning heart attacks

- Laughter can also provide a safe, non-threatening way to shift blocked feelings and emotions that, over time, can lead to mental and physical stress and depression. (Many's the time as a social worker that I sat with bereaved relatives who, in between tears, had us all laughing out loud as they related funny stories about their loved one)

And here's one added extra in case you're still on the fence about having a bit of a laugh. A University of Pennsylvania research study[32] found that *playfulness makes both men and women more attractive to the opposite sex!*

Ten Tips for Creating Optimism at WorK

A word of caution: ease into this if you haven't built trust or earned the right. A bit like after twenty years of a 'flowerless' partnership, suddenly turning up with flowers – too much, too soon and people are likely to become suspicious of your motives for suddenly wanting to 'play'.

1. Create a positive environment for yourself and others. No more BMWs and definitely no red socks. Steer clear of negative people who'll suck your energy like a vampire.

2. Get to know and play to everyone's strengths.

3. As far as possible quarantine yourselves from the constant stream of bad news we're exposed to almost hourly now. Check out some of the good news websites, read inspirational blogs and stories.

4. Use the mood meter to build your EQ and track your moods. Remember, if you're the boss, your mood is highly contagious.

5. Focus on what you *can* do about something when adversity strikes, rather than ruminating on what's now effectively history and can't be changed.

6. Reframe, reframe, reframe. Change your perspective, change your thinking and change your mood.

7. Try Marty Seligman's free optimism survey and many others at https://www.authentichappiness.sas. upenn.edu/testcenter

---

32 - *Adult Play and Sexual Selection*, Dr. Garry Chick, Pennsylvania State University Scholarpedia, 2013

8. Start to keep track of your internal critic and the self-chat you allow to drift through your brain, as well as what you say out loud. It all impacts what your brain takes on board and acts on. Have a read of your emails too and do a bit of hygiene check for pessimistic versus optimistic language.

9. Volunteer, do stuff for free, help people out – it will give you a dopamine and oxytocin kick.

10. Play. If you're not sure how to play at work, there are many websites with ideas of simple, no or low cost, non-naff things you can do at work. One website for you to check out: http://www.deepfun.com/playing-together-for-fun-creative-play-and-lifelong-games

11. <u>BONUS TIP</u> – If people, including your manager, are in any doubt, let them know what the health (and possibly romance!) benefits are of lightening up a bit.

And finally, if you're looking for more creative, catalytic and innovative ideas at work, then you absolutely need to 'get your play on'. Fact is when people become overly serious, when they're in a pessimistic, command and control, zero-tolerance-for-mistakes kind of culture, it's hardly going to be any surprise that they'll stick to the letter of law. They'll keep their heads down, struggle with any sort of ambiguity, won't dare to take any initiative, and, as Marty Seligman found, will learn to be helpless, waiting for you to tell them what to do.

Yikes! Let me out of there!

COACH AND MENTOR

- TIME TO 'GET YOUR COACH ON' AND THRIVE

- CELEBRATING THE GOOD (and what to do when the wheels get a bit wobbly)

Chapter 9

TIME TO 'GET YOUR COACH ON' AND THRIVE

If Positive Psychology teaches us anything it's that
all of us are a mixture of strengths and weaknesses.
No one has it all, and no one lacks it all.

Christopher Peterson

I had a bit of writer's block when I got to this chapter and so, entering into the spirit of the tortured creative, I lay awake until well after midnight, back of hand on brow, pen and paper next to me in the dark and pondered. Then it came to me …

This chapter is all about developing yourself and developing your people. That includes coaching and developing people around things like:

- Knowing and playing to personal strengths, so people get into a state of peak performance known as 'flow'

- Challenging a mindset or set of beliefs that's maybe holding someone back from being the best they can be

- Supporting people as they step out of their comfort zone, flex their strength muscles and grow

What I realised is that I can't actually recall anyone ever doing much of that with me once I moved into the corporate world. And sad to say again that if the engagement research is anything to go by, many of you probably haven't experienced much of this kind of development or coaching either.

Oh yes, I was frequently psych tested within an inch of my life prior to being offered a job, as potential employers tried to work out if what they saw was in fact what they might be getting. But here's the weird and frankly baffling thing. Having confirmed that I was in fact the real deal, jobs were offered, I accepted, and then, in the main, people got on with trying to make me the same as everyone else, in one bewildering and confidence shattering case, promptly hanging me out to dry.

Maybe it's just me, but that seems like some kind of crazy …

Remember all that stuff about core purpose I talked about in Chapter 4? One of the clues to finding core purpose is this: think about those things or situations that get you fired up, when you've found yourself speaking out, perhaps risked your job or a relationship, because you can't, no, you won't sit still and allow whatever it is to happen. At times like this, it's highly likely that your reaction is because the situation is deeply at odds with your core purpose and your values.

Given my core purpose, nothing gets me more fired up than talking to people and finding out they're living lives of quiet desperation, going through the motions day by day, eking out a living to pay the bills. All that human potential going unrecognised. Tragedy all round, far as I'm concerned, and the reason companies don't thrive and profits don't grow.

Quite often you're going to find that people are blind to their strengths.They find it hard to figure out or say what their strengths actually are, or to talk about them clearly. This is important, so I'll say it again – the bottom line is if you're going to build and sustain a thriving team and a profitable company, getting your head around your own and everyone else's strengths is the place to start.

I'm going to talk about coaching and developing people shortly so just a quick reminder of those figures I quoted earlier in *Culture 101 – in organisations that managed people to or overly focused on weaknesses performance dropped by 26.8%. By comparison, companies that focused on, managed and developed people to their strengths, showed an increase in performance of 36%.*

Want more specifics on how that might benefit you, your team and the company? Along with decades of Gallup Research[33], leading researchers in the strengths and Positive Psychology space like Robert Biswas-Diener, Todd Kashdan and Gurpal Minhas[34] found several, hard to argue with outcomes of managing people to their strengths:

- The use of strengths is a core predictor of workplace engagement

- Workplace engagement increases when people develop realised and/or unrealised strengths

- Business leaders who focus on developing themselves on the basis of strengths are more effective

---

33 - *How* Employees' Strengths Make Your Company Stronger, Susan Sorenson, Gallup, February 20, 2014
34 - *A Dynamic Approach to Psychological Strength Development and Intervention*, Robert Biswas-Diener, Todd Kashdan and Gurpal Minhas, The Journal of Positive Psychology, March 2011

Strengths, Achieving Goals and Flow

The best advice I could give anyone is to spend your time working on whatever you are passionate about in life.

Richard Branson

In recent times, if the proliferation of adult colouring-in books is anything to go by, there's been quite a surge of interest in certain forms of what I call yoga for the mind. Things to do that cause your brain to focus on the present moment, block out other incoming information – activities that are basically aimed at calming your mind and giving your stressed out brain a bit of a rest (sort of like meditation on the run for people who find actual meditation a bit too woo-woo).

All good stuff but, as research scientists have discovered, there's a bit more to mindfulness and getting into what's called a state of flow than some pencils and a colouring-in book, or popping on your happy pants and lying on a yoga mat.

So, there is indeed this thing called flow, nothing to do with water, unless of course that's your area of passion.

Ever recall a time when you were doing something, either at work, a hobby or sport, something you really enjoy doing and are good at – using your natural strengths and skills, taking it up a notch, feeling a bit challenged – and time just seemed to sort of fade away? You got so lost in the activity, so focused that you became oblivious to much of what was going on around you? I've got into flow several times while writing this book, only to look up and realise several hours had passed because the sun had gone down and I needed to turn on the lights.

Flow is about those moments when, using your natural skills or strengths, you're engaged in doing something that's an 'above average' challenge for you, and so you need to step it up a notch or two and use your skills at an above average level. Even though they're keen to win events, elite athletes for example, talk a lot about beating their PB – personal best – the very definition of flow.

Mihaly Csikszentmihalyi (he suggested pronouncing it chicks-sent-me-high, works for me) was one of the leading researchers around the concept of flow and, interestingly, what he and others found is that *as long as we're using our strengths*, our natural skills and talents, we're far more likely to experience flow at work than in our leisure time. 'Control of consciousness determines the quality of life … flow … is characterised by complete absorption in what one does.' [35]

Think about that for a moment. When you're at work, if your job is a good match for your strengths, you'll be using your natural skills and talents and improving them, as long as you have projects that challenge you without tipping you over the edge. Too much challenge and you're likely to start getting anxious and end up in confidence-crushing failure; too little and, well, boredom sets in. And even if you do love doing something, the same old constant repetition is a bit of a buzz-killer too – remember, one of our drives is to get better at what we love doing, aiming for mastery.

For most of us – and there's no judgement here folks – our leisure time is spent in more passive activities like watching the box, watching a sport or looking at artworks or a play, for example, rather than being an active participant, plus we don't tend to have the kind of deadlines we have at work to spur us on. So, on the weekends, or indeed when many people retire, we're not actually using our skills and strengths – unless of course you fill your after work hours or

---

35 - *Flow: The Psychology of Optimal Experience*, Mihaly Csikszentmihalyi, Harper Perennial, 1990

retirement with the relentless pursuit of excellence in some kind of hobby or sport.

Flow has very good press too – like all the other keys to a thriving culture I've talked about. When people are in a state of flow for long periods of time, they report feeling happier, healthier, more creative, more self-confident and more satisfied.

Makes me wonder, again, what's going on with those mind-numbingly shocking engagement scores. An epidemic, I'm thinking, of people not using or developing their strengths at work. Arghhhh!

You see, when you've got people doing stuff day in, day out, that's been dropped on them from a great height post multiple restructures or redundancies, it's highly likely they're way 'off-piste'. Or maybe they've taken a job for the great money being offered (made that mistake myself – twice – never again), or because it's the norm to be promoted into whatever job they've found themselves in (case in point: the top sales person who got promoted into the sales manager job – might work out, might not), or because they just really needed a job. And yes, I'm a realist; there's possibly going to be times when that's a harsh reality.

Yet you can pretty much guarantee that, in these situations, people aren't doing anything remotely linked to their 'why', their core purpose, which, as you now know, is a soul-destroying highway to feeling disconnected, as you're now helping someone else achieve *their* goals while your own get left behind in the dust.

The thing is it's inevitable that there are going to be tasks in any job that sap energy, don't come naturally, are a weakness rather than a strength, but still need to be done. An artist needs to sell their artwork to make a living from their passion; a café owner who loves front of house still needs to do the books; I need to write detailed facilitator instructions (detail's not a strengths for me).

If people are underperforming, chances are that they're in overwhelm because the task is way too challenging for their existing skills set, or they're bored witless because it doesn't challenge them enough. Get the balance between challenge, support and skill level right and voila – you've got flow.

Here's the 'a-ha' – remember from Chapter 4 that it's been found even the toughest jobs will get done, even things that don't make us happy in the moment, *if* you've done the groundwork, for you and your team, on meaning and purpose. With purpose as the anchor, part of your work in coaching people is in helping them to see how they can draw on a strength to get through the challenging tasks and days.

Yes siree, it all comes full-circle.

So, there are indeed powerful links between purpose, strengths, flow, achieving goals and, ultimately, a company's productivity and profitability and with the kinds of conversations you have with your team.

The Human Spine Decalcifier (Otherwise Known as The Annual Performance Review)

Remember the Gallup Big Six? One of the things your Millennials (and most likely the rest of your peeps) are looking for is an ongoing, more informal, regular check-in conversation with you. *Not* a quarterly or annual performance review – at best a tick box exercise with your pay rise or promotion possibly at risk; at worst a chance for the boss to highlight your deficiencies with impunity thus skewering any chance of a pay rise or promotion, activating your fight or flight bouncers, along with that neurological pathway for rejection, the same one as for physical pain. Great state to be in as you discuss your future …

(I once had a manager tell me to fill in her responses as well as mine. Gee whiz, such affirmation of my worth …)

About those annual performance reviews: why, oh why are you still doing them?

Believe me, I'm more than willing to be convinced if someone can show me evidence of some kind of annual performance review system that has, as I said in the opening of *Culture 101,* regularly resulted in positive, ground-breaking, catalytic, career-defining epiphanies for everyone concerned. Anyone?

Enough about my thoughts; what exactly do other people think of performance reviews?[36]

- 66% of employees said the performance review process interferes with their productivity

- 65% say it isn't relevant to their jobs

- 90% of HR professionals don't believe their companies performance reviews provide accurate information

- 95% of managers aren't satisfied with their organisation's performance management and review process

The list of companies who've dumped the formal review process in favour of something more conducive to human thriving is impressive and growing – Yahoo, Accenture, Microsoft, Cigna, Deloitte and General Electric. They've all reported not only measureable positive outcomes, but in Deloitte's case they estimated it's saved them two million hours of lost time per year.

'Nuff said.

---

36 - *Is it Time to Put the Performance Review on a PIP*, Dori Meinert, Society for Human Resource Management, April 2015

A Mind for Thriving

A lot of people are aware that there's a link between what goes on in our heads, the old self-talk, and the results we want and do get, or those goals we miss – often repeatedly.

A bit like the Pygmalion Effect I talked about earlier, where the attitude or perceptions of other people can affect our behaviour, there are times, I'm sure, when many of us don't need much outside help in that department.

Let's divert again into some brain science to get some perspective on just how powerful that internal chat is and how it can impact your life in weird and sometimes wonderful ways.

Some years ago, I heard a fascinating story back when I thought being a pharmacist was the way for me to go – yes, I know, I was waaaaaaaaaaaay off. Nonetheless, I had an absolute ball. It was my first co-ed experience after being at all-girls schools for ten years. I found I loved physics and anatomy but hated chemistry (bit of a problem if you want to be a chemist) and learnt some very interesting things. One of those interesting things was about the incredible power of placebos.

Dr David Hamilton left medical research in 1999 after spending four years in drug development, and began researching and writing books on the link between our minds, our beliefs and our bodies. He'd been gob-smacked, when working on clinical trials for new drugs, at the incredible effectiveness of placebos – basically sugar pills containing absolutely no drug at all.

'In (**one study**) 40 asthmatics were given an inhaler containing a placebo that was just water vapour, but they were told that it contained allergens that would restrict their airways. Nineteen of them went on to suffer considerable constriction of their airways. Twelve of them actually experienced a full-blown asthma attack. When they were given a different inhaler and told it would relieve their symptoms, it did, even though it was also a placebo. One person in the study even developed symptoms of hay fever after being told that the inhaler also contained pollen.'[37]

Even more studies showed that 'patients given placebos experience biochemical changes that improve their condition. Placebo painkillers activate the body's natural analgesics. Parkinson's placebos prompt the brain to release dopamine; anxiety and depression placebos elicit changes in the areas of the brain that regulate emotion. One particularly remarkable study recruited patients with irritable-bowel syndrome and told them that their treatment would be 'pills made of an inert substance, like sugar pills, that have been shown in clinical studies to produce significant improvement in IBS symptoms through mind-body, self-healing processes'. Even though the treatment was a placebo, and even though the patients *knew* it was a placebo, they showed significant improvement'[38].

Conversely, researchers have also found the nocebo effect, where, if people have a negative expectation of a side effect or are given a profoundly negative prognosis, then they're far more likely to experience those effects, and live or die to that prognosis.

Pretty compelling evidence that our minds are indeed amazing, and, given certain information, can outwit even the strongest of pain and potentially heal us, or not.

So, what does this mean for coaching your team, for dealing with areas where you too might be experiencing less than ideal results and for building a thriving culture?

Each of us have our own internal (but often quite noisy!) version of a variety of self-limiting mindsets that run

37 - *The Amazing Power of The Placebo*, Dr. David R. Hamilton Ph.D., November 2012
38 - *The Nocebo Effect: How We Worry Ourselves Sick*, Gareth Cook, The New Yorker, March 29 2013

interference from time to time, setting up us in a bit of a failure loop around certain subject areas and making it hard to achieve goals.

The upshot of this kind of mindset is ultimately giving up, giving in, convinced there's no wriggle room, no chance of changing or opportunity for growth of any kind. And the lack of improvement or failure just becomes proof positive of our internal critic's 'see I told you so, buster' view of your potential around that particular subject.

For a lot of people who aren't getting the results they want, or say they want, it can be a bit of a mystery to get your head around what needs to change to make sure you get something better going on in the results department.

If, for example, you've been bit of a yoyo dieter, or a have goal achievement record that's worthy of a Swiss Alps topography map, have a think for a moment about what happens when you decide to lose weight or go for that sales goal.

Most people, with absolutely the best of intentions, make some kind of statement about what they're aiming for, then get very gung-ho about changing their behaviour – low carbs, join a gym, even lay down some serious hard-earned on fancy new cross trainers. Maybe, preparing to launch their new business campaign, they've agreed to a bullish stretch sales target, then analysed, prepared, researched and even presented a proposal or five, or six, or seven …

Excellent, go get 'em tiger for a few weeks, or maybe even only days, until the old habits creep in and off the yoyo goes again in the other direction. And yet they seemed so definite about really wanting the goal this time!

So, what just happened and, in all likelihood, will keep happening?

Please – step away from the scales, put the gym membership on hold, no more client calls for a week or so and maybe, just maybe, consider something different.

Carol Dweck from Stanford University has spent years researching what kind of mindset holds people back from achieving more and what gets the juices flowing and challenges overcome. What emerged, captured in her book *Mindset*[39], is what she refers to as the difference between a 'fixed' mindset – seeing talent or skill as something you either have or don't have in that area of your life – and a 'growth' mindset – where people embrace a challenge, stretch themselves and see few if any limits on learning new skills. As Dweck say, 'The passion for stretching yourself and sticking to it, even (or especially) when it's not going well, is the hallmark of the growth mindset. This is the mindset that allows people to thrive during some of the most challenging times in their lives'.

What Can You Do as a Coach When People are Stuck?

- Watch your mouth. Tough love, I know. But I encourage you to tune in to what you say and what others are saying when goals aren't being hit or challenges avoided. What's said inside your head or out loud to others is not only having a powerful impact on your brain, it's also firming up your limiting and fixed mindset.

- Look, read and listen to the messages you and the company send out. Are people getting a message that says they have permanent fixed traits that are being measured to some pre-defined high-performers, 'gold' standard? Or are you and the company sending messages about being genuinely interested in helping them develop as a person?

---

39 - *Mindset: The New Psychology of Success*, Carol S. Dweck, Ph.D., Ballantine Books, 2006

- In areas where a desired outcome continues to be a slippery little sucker, get them to sit down and write out what their limiting beliefs are for that area of work or life. Of course, you need to have built trust here because you want the real truth, warts and all. I promise it'll be very illuminating when you do and will give you and them something to use your reframing muscles on.

- What's your tolerance for mistakes? Are you still trying to motivate by fear of negative outcomes? (Good luck with that … remember back to those heart surgery patients.)

- When people are in a growth frame of mind, mistakes are inevitable. What happens next is in a large part up to your reaction.

- When you hear yourself or your people say, 'I can't do it', get your coach on, treat people as the amazing individuals they are and say, 'Not yet'.

Coaching to Thrive

Ask anyone about coaching and goals and, at some point, S.M.A.R.T[40] goals will probably pop up, along with G.R.O.W,[41] which I describe as a sort of road map for an effective coaching chat. All are good, and most definitely have their place, especially at the sharp end of coaching. Yet, seems to me there are often some critical things missing from the front end of the discussion.

Fact is we are funny creatures, us humans. It's kind of like when you look at the earth from outer space. From far away, neat and tidy, a big blue planet. But zoom in, fly drone-close over the earth or do a bit of a David Attenborough, and things look very different. There are highs and lows, smooth bits and sharp; it's messy, pristine, beautiful and treacherous, loud and soft. Humans are a bit the same.

---

40 - Specific Measurable Achievable Realistic and Time bound
41 - Goals Reality Options and Will Do, (devised by John Whitmore)

Until you really get to know someone, it's all a bit squeaky clean, tidy, put together, quirks tucked away, no insecurities, the 'it's all good', 'game face on' work image. The reality is, up close, when we build trust and get to know someone, we might actually be given the privilege of seeing the real person, goodies, quirks and all. And sometimes, when we earn that right, we might get to see some deeply buried, well-hidden gems that no one has seen for quite some time, quite possibly including the 'owner' of those gems.

Often I hear about people earnestly, and with the best of intentions, launching into a coaching conversation without having much idea about the person sitting opposite them, what makes them tick, what their dreams and aspirations are. And yet often the person they're coaching is about to make a decision, possibly an expensive one if, for example, it involves tertiary education or a career move, that could affect the rest of their life, or a fair chunk of it.

(In my coaching work, I've met people of all ages, from Millennials to Boomers, who are utterly miserable because of a decision about their career that they made – or in some cases was made for them by well-meaning parents – when they were in their late teens at school.)

And yetm when you think about it, there's so much at stake here – basic happiness and lifelong fulfillment, for a start.

So, when you're sitting down and working out individual goals with your people, then coaching and developing them, here's a few tips to make sure you set everyone up for success.

Before They Join the Team

- Recruit people for strengths using a tool like the Strengths Profile from CAPP

- Ask questions when you're interviewing to check the alignment with your company core purpose (for example, ask them to 'tell us about something you've done that demonstrates living one of our values')

Coaching and Developing the Team

- Clarify and make explicit their core purpose and the individual meaning and connection to company core purpose

- If they haven't already done it, get people to complete the Strengths Profile

- Do some team sessions with someone accredited, using the Strengths Profile, V.I.A, or tools like the Myers Briggs Type Indicator or DiSC

- Agree on goals aligned to each person's dreams using the tips on goal setting

- Assign tasks and goals that get them into flow as often as possible

- Talk through strategies on how they'll handle the less 'sexy' but necessary stuff

- Coach them by way of regular, planned, informal check-in chats

- Listen; give them the gift of your attention

- Ask questions to check in for a limiting belief or a fixed mindset, watch what you say and listen for words indicating a fixed mindset

- Use these two simple yet powerful words – **not yet** – to encourage a growth mindset in yourself and your team (try saying it now to one of your own discouraging fixed mindset live chats and see what happens to your thinking – what you'll usually find is your brain, seeing a disconnect, will automatically start searching for new ideas and information. Cool!)

And, finally, make sure on a regular basis, that you encourage people using 'growth mindset' words, and give recognition where recognition is due – the subject of the next chapter.

Chapter 10

CELEBRATING THE GOOD STUFF (and what to do when the wheels get a bit wobbly)

> I have yet to find a man, however exalted his
> station, who did not do better work and put forth
> greater effort under a spirit of approval than
> under a spirit of criticism.
>
> **Charles Schwab**

Have to tell you, it's good therapy writing a book, dredging up some weird but true stories from the past, having an often times incredulous laugh about some of them with friends, and then exorcising some demons that may have had a bit of a hold and possibly temporarily rerouted a growth mindset or two …

One of those demonic stories happened back in my recruiting days, where, after it all had started out well, I was now three years into the job and often cried on the way to work, but at the same time, was scared of leaving because of the impact of that 'recession we had to have'.

I was a lot younger then and pretty naïve, especially about the corporate world, but despite a boss who had never coached or developed me and who regularly took credit for what I'd done (including my year-long campaign to have a Federal Minister present at a 500-person sold out client function), I'd been very successful and was regarded as one of the go-to people for recruitment expertise in my space.

One morning, my boss's boss invited me to come have a chat. I was over the moon! In three years, he'd barely spoken to me and this was on the back of my having just won a five year Australian contract with one of world's largest companies. So, I grabbed my pen and paper, practically skipped into the room and waited breathlessly for what was to come. (Whoa, as I'm typing this I just got a hit of adrenaline as my bouncers checked 'the door list'. This little incident is very much on the 'no-fly' list so I've just been given a shot across the bow from my amygdalae – which have veeeeeery long memories …)

After the obligatory pleasantries, here's sort of how it went (and I swear, I *am not* making this stuff up):

Him: (looking slightly uncomfortable) Umm … ah … umm … you know how when you win a client you're very happy and you talk about it and let people know?

Me: (slightly puzzled as not quite sure where things were going): Yeeeeess?

Him: (looking a bit more uncomfortable) Well … umm … err … what we've (note the collective 'we', so my paranoia now starts to kick in as me and my amygdalae start to wonder who's been talking about me – one guess) noticed is that when you umm … umm … don't win a proposal, you're not so happy …

Me: (brow even more furrowed) Yeeeeess?

Him: (panic-stricken by now) Umm … umm … umm … well, ah, from now on we'd like you to (both hands now at elbow height, palms down as he moved them horizontally back and forth), umm, sort of, umm, err … umm … (as the hands continued their horizontal window wiping)

Me: (with a slight edge of disbelief and an attempt at humour to break the tension) You want me to sort of flat-line, is that it?

Him: (with evident relief) Yes! Yes, great! That's it, that's a great way of putting it, flat-line.

Me: (teeth gritted now to stop the tears) So, what you're really saying is that you all want me to flat-line?

Him: (off the hook now) Yep, yep, that's it. That would be great!

As you know, I've worked in A & E and ICU and, if you've watched any of *Greys' Anatomy*, well, I think we all know what flat-line means – you're dead. I'm still shaking my head in disbelief almost 25 years later.

What did I do then? Well, I'm more your flight kind of person rather than a fighter or a freezer. So, I quietly took off out of the building, walked around that huge city block three times, and finally, though I'm not a religious person, ended up in a city church where I sat in quiet contemplation and utter disbelief, and took in what had just happened. Bang, bang, you're dead.

Now, I've mentioned too that I can be a bit of a drama queen at times (bit of a clue right there in that last line). And as anyone who is one too (you know who you are), who's married to one or has managed one, you know that we feel things; I mean *really* feel things.

We tend to score high on the empathy scale, a critical trait in any situation where you need to understand and 'enter the world' of another person – like sales, acting, coaching or counselling, for example.

It's a strength and, like any strength, that's mostly great in the right circumstances and when you're with people who've taken the time to get to know you, who appreciate your gifts, who 'get you' and want to get the best out of you. But sometimes, just like any other overused strength, it can be a bit over the top if it's not the appropriate style for the people around you, or it ends up being a bit too much of a good thing.

Time, distance and a few years of 'therapy' later, I can see where he wanted to go with his misguided observations (I know … let it go, Pen, let it go …). He wasn't, to my knowledge, a psychopath who actually wanted me dead, and his intentions no doubt were good – but the execution and the delivery of his message totally sucked.

Especially as, apart from the 'won-them-because-you-hit-the-targets' awards, there hadn't been any other regular, significant, personal recognition, no praise, encouragement or individual development, and certainly no deposits in my emotional bank account, as Steven Covey[42] aptly named it. So, he'd just made one big, massive withdrawal.

(When it comes to the how of building trust, I love Steven Covey's idea that each of us has an emotional bank account. If you want to build trust with anyone then you need to make deposits in their emotional bank account by doing some of the things I've been talking about – listen to me; catch me doing something right; give me genuine, heartfelt clear, timely recognition and corrective feedback; coach and mentor me; take a genuine interest in me as an individual and help me get to know and use my strengths – that's a few good places to start.)

---

42 - *The Seven Habits of Highly Effective People*, Steven Covey, FreePress, 1989

Let's look at the science behind recognition, how to do recognition, and why you need to do it genuinely and often.

Recognition and Positive Feedback

What it's like to be recognised, to be seen, to have someone's attention, to have them be 'present' for you is another one of those easy-to-do free things that travels to the brain's 'reward' centre and gives the person on the receiving end a hit of that wonderful stuff called dopamine.

Remember, dopamine is also involved in addictive behaviour, and not all addictive behaviour is bad for us! On the plus side, when you and your team add in giving each other regular, genuine recognition and encouragement to your growing armoury of thriving culture tools, you're building real and lasting engagement. Fundamentally, as one of my Positive Psychology lecturers said, 'If you have a place in your life where you get this, you'll go back there'.

Frankly, I've always been baffled by how reluctant some people are to give praise, positive feedback or recognition, or to be happy for others when they have a win or some good news.

I'm not talking here about pumping up someone's tyres or giving them a big head. Just letting them know that you're proud of them, recognise the effort they're making, that they've persisted through hardships perhaps, or acknowledging achievement or good news. I used to think it was a case of tall poppy syndrome, which used to be thought to be a particularly Aussie behaviour, and possibly a more male thing to do, too. But it's a bit more widespread than that; in fact, it happens across the gender spectrum and many if not most cultures. What is that about?

Science it seems has confirmed something that we've intuitively known that 'negative occurrences bad events and disapproving feedback were more influential and longer lasting in individuals than positive, encouraging and upbeat occurrences'.[43]

Think about that for a moment. I know for me and many other facilitators that when we read the 'happy sheets' (otherwise known as evaluations) at the end of a program, all the positive feedback from, say, 15 participants will fade into insignificance while we ruminate on the one piece of negative feedback (sometimes from the one person who was determined to maintain their disenchantment at being 'voluntold' to attend, their hostage stance, to the end), often very useful constructive criticism and well-founded.

As you might've guessed, this focus on the negative has got a lot to do with survival, with those days of wandering the Savannah looking for food. On our daily scrounge for sustenance, keeping an eye out for any clear and present danger was obviously critical for survival. We basically evolved with a sort of 'what's wrong with this picture' take on the world, looking for the negatives, what's not working. Bit like some of the places many of us seem to have worked in, and, unfortunately, maybe still do.

Ignore something negative like a deep, low growl, or nowadays say a smoke alarm, and your life's in danger. On the other hand, miss out on seeing an amazing sunset, the fireworks or going to a party and, while you might regret missing it, it's not going to have any long-term negative consequences for your survival.

Take that into the workplace when companies hear the news of a catalytic competitor innovation, significant market, customer or product changes or other unforeseen threats, and you can see how easy it is to drop into a focusing-on-the-negative,   catching-people-doing-something-wrong type of culture. The collective amygdalae are grumbling and on alert as a threat to the company's survival is perceived.

---

43 - Bad is Stronger Than Good, Baeumeister, R.F., Bratslavsky, E., Finkenauer, C., Vohs, K.D., Review of General Psychology, 5 (4), 2001

The outcome of course is that your people will go into a fight or flight state, just at the very time you need them to be most creative, collaborative and focused.

Positive events and the accompanying hormone hits are also waaaaaay faster and more fleeting than the impact of negative events – blink and you miss it – and we tend not to think about or ruminate (in a good way) on positive events for anywhere near as long as the negative events. Hence, we're effectively missing out on the amazing knock-on effect on our brains and our creative ability, as found by Barbara Fredrickson[44] in her Broaden and Build theory mentioned earlier.

Take a moment here. Put the book down and think about your last significant holiday. Have a free dopamine and serotonin hit on me – you're welcome!

Back in the day, people used to have get-togethers that went something like this. Unsuspecting friends and neighbours were invited over for a casserole (or fondue if you were really cool), and before you could down your first red/green-cocktail-onion-lump-of-cheddar-cheese on a stick, the projector was whipped out and the 'slide night' began. Slide after slide went by, as the hosts basked in the dopamine and serotonin glow of reminiscing about their most recent holiday. Boring for the unwitting audience maybe but a great way to re-experience some powerfully positive events.

Typically today, there's the mandatory holiday posts on Insta and that's about it. People rarely, if ever, get the chance to relive their wonderful holiday experience, with all the accompanying dopamine hits, and, frankly, often get the sense that no one really seems remotely interested (or is maybe a teeny bit jealous?). And while this mightn't seem to be all that important, as you'll see, how we react to people's

---

44 - *Positivity; Ground Breaking Research to Release Your Inner Optimist and Thrive* Barbara Fredrickson, Oneworld, 2009

good news, achievements, or successes is one of the most significant aspects of recognition.

Here are some more 'fun facts' from that 50 years' worth of Gallup data[45]:

- The **number-one reason people** leave their jobs: they don't feel appreciated

- **65%** of people received no recognition in the workplace in the last year leading to them feeling negative and unappreciated (funny that)

- **Negative employees** can scare off **every** customer they speak with, for good

- **Nine out of ten** people say they are more productive when they're around **positive people**

- The magic ratio: **five** positive interactions for every **one** negative interaction/piece of constructive criticism

Those last numbers, by the way, are grounded in yet more research.

Barbara Fredrickson did some further work collaborating with Marcial Losada, a mathematician who contacted her because he'd come up with a mathematical formula for her Broaden and Build theory. Losada and his team had done years of scientific research on high-performing teams looking at three aspects of face-to-face communication. In meetings, the research teams observed the following things – were people's statements 1) positive or negative? 2) self or other focused? 3) based on inquiring (asking questions) or advocacy (defending a point of view)?

---

45 - *How Full is Your Bucket*, Tom Rath and Donald Clifton Gallup Press, 2004

The long and short of it is that not unlike another researcher, John Gottman (who, with his wife, works in the field of couples' relationships), what Losada and his team found 'led to his prediction that only when positivity ratios are higher than three to one is positivity in sufficient supply to seed human flourishing'.[46]

By the way, while recognition is one way to build up your 3:1's during the day, the point the researchers make is that it's about anything said, done or communicated that leads to people feeling a positive emotion – even fleetingly.

Here's a little summary[47] of some of the frankly mind-blowing effects of having at least a 3:1 positivity ratio:

- People live longer (+11 years)

- People succumb to fewer illnesses

- People stay married longer

- People tolerate pain better

- People work harder

- People perform better on the job

- People make more money (+30%)

- People display more mental acuity

- People make higher quality decisions

- People are more creative and flexible in their thinking

- People are more adaptive and resilient after trials and traumas

- People engage in more helping behaviours and citizenship activities

---

46 - *Positivity: Ground Breaking Research to Release Your Inner Optimist and Thrive* Barbara Fredrickson, Oneworld, 2009
47 - Positive Leadership: Strategies for Extraordinary Performance, Kim Cameron, Berrett-Koehler, 2012

This seemingly simple little ratio then, 3:1, is your way to build trust, build your deposits in the emotional bank accounts of your team and is what will earn you the right to give harder-to-hear feedback to someone without a full-blown amygdala blow up, during the tougher times at work, or when, like any leader, you have to let people down because it's just not possible for you to know everything, or when you're not able to do something for them.

If you haven't built trust over time, made those deposits, then well-intentioned constructive feedback will very likely come across, understandably, as something of an ambush to the person on the other end – as I experienced all those years ago. Fight or flight, here we come.

Practise how you'll give recognition following the tips at the end of the chapter, because recognition and praise has an even shorter shelf life than a pack of Tim Tams in the staff fridge. What neuroscience tells us is 'recognition has the largest effect on trust when it occurs immediately after a goal has been achieved, when it comes from peers, and when it's tangible, unexpected, personal and public'. [48]

Good News – Make It Matter

> Doing anything good in this place is like taking a pee in a wetsuit … makes you feel warm all over but no one knows or cares about it …
>
> **Anonymous**

So, basic recognition is important, 3:1 type of important. But what about when people have a big win, some really good news or a significant success?

---

48 - *The Neuroscience of Trust*, Paul J. Zak, Harvard Business Review, January/ February 2017

Another couple of researchers, Gable and Gonzaga,[49] found that there are four typical ways people will respond to positive news:

- Active Constructive – 'Shut the front door! You did what! That's amazing! Let me save this work, then I want you to sit down and tell me all about it!'

- Passive Constructive – 'That's nice for you dear, glad it worked out.'

- Active Destructive – 'And how much is that going to cost me? Terrific, thanks a lot – not.'

- Passive Destructive – 'Oh. Aren't we the lucky one, again.'

Active constructive is the only type of response that works on building a relationship. In fact, the researchers found it was a much stronger predictor of relationship longevity, work or otherwise, than the type of support given to people during tough times.

Let that soak in for a minute, and think about your closest relationships – like my lecturer said: if you're getting this kind of recognition and support somewhere, you're going to go back there.

Gable and Gonzaga use the word 'capitalisation' to describe the impact of active constructive responses to positive events in someone's life. Effectively, when someone decides to share their good news with you, an active constructive response is like a mini personal 'slide night', setting off the good hormone hits, and in the long run it leads to far greater relationship satisfaction, higher engagement and

---

49 - *Will You Be There for Me When Things Go Right? Supportive Responses to Positive Event Disclosures*, S. L. Gable and G.C. Gonzaga, Journal of Personality and Social Psychology Vol. 91, No.5., 2006

less communication misunderstandings. Funny, I've always referred to recognition as being the glue of good, solid, long-lasting relationships, and receiving it being a bit like a much-needed blood transfusion. Now I know why!

Three important engagement-building things happen when we're on the receiving end of active constructive listening, things that work for me, and I'm sure for you:

- Understanding – you get me

- Validation – you think I'm okay

- Caring – you care about me

Finally, remember that when a response is actively or passively destructive (someone feeling threatened or jealous maybe?) the neural pathway for social rejection, the same as for physical pain, gets fired up.

Any wonder then that people who feel undervalued, unrecognised and unappreciated soon debunk to somewhere else – basically to stop the pain.

The 'How To' of Recognition

Recognition, real genuine, personalised recognition is a bit more than a 'thanks mate, well done'. Thanks for what exactly? What did I do well? Throwaway comments like that aren't specific; there's no genuine expression of appreciation for a 'beyond-the-call-of-duty' type of action or success, and they end up feeling like lip service.

If someone's done something you're really happy about, that you want them to do again, then think back to when you trained your last puppy, if you've ever had one.

Basic behavioural psychology: reward behaviour that you want to continue. So, minus the liver treats, we're much the same as that puppy. Our reward centre gets fired up when we get real recognition; the dopamine hit feels good and is addictive (in a good way) so we're more likely to repeat whatever we got rewarded for!

When I talk about recognition, I often get all sorts of reasons thrown up as to why someone can't do it or might not want to receive it. Fascinating.

Here's a select few: 'I'm too busy … I'll embarrass them … I'll give them a big head … They'll expect it all the time … It's too touch feely for them/me … They're being paid, what else do they need?…Surely they can work it out for themselves without me pointing it out'. Wow! Quite the reaction, all for suggesting it might be an idea to give people some positive feedback, especially given the staggering rewards for everyone concerned as Gallup and others have found!

Firstly, the research tells us that even the most introverted of souls, who recoil in horror at the very thought of public praise, will thrive on an appropriate dialed-down form of recognition.

Secondly – too busy? Really? Too busy doing what exactly? It's pretty hard to argue with that Gallup research from 4 million people demonstrating that this is one of the simplest and easiest things you can do, regularly, that can have a massive impact on your bottom line, amongst other things.

If it's not already, showing your people you appreciate them needs to move to the top of your to-do list.

As for the flowery, touch-feely comments I get, a good, focused recognition spiel takes less than twenty seconds and doesn't have to be a sick-making exercise in sugar coated fluff. Example: 'Thanks so much for the time you put into that report. So well thought out and had exactly the result I needed with finance. I know you were here 'til late without so much as a grumble – you've got such a can-do attitude – and you made me look like a hero.Thanks again'.

Tips for a Focused Recognition Statement

- Be specific in naming exactly what it was they did so they're really clear on what you're recognising or praising. Mention who they helped out (e.g. you, the team, the company, a customer, or another area of the business).

- What problem did they solve or help out with? How did they go about doing it? What was their attitude?

- How did it benefit people?

- Make sure your words are memorable. No one's going to remember 'Well done buddy'. Be creative and genuine. 'Pure genius … You totally rocked that presentation … You are the bomb when it comes to financials,' or, 'I would have missed this if you hadn't picked it up'. It doesn't have to be elaborate, just genuine and specific.

- Once you've delivered the praise, leave the person to bask in the glow of dopamine for a while. Doing this also underlines the importance of the recognition. Follow it straight away with something about business or a project and you've diluted the moment.

… and if You Do Have To Have a Difficult 'Fireside Chat' …

Here's the thing. For the vast majority of the population, people simply don't get out of bed every morning, regardless of their role, and decide every day that today's mission is to make life miserable for everyone, to make mistakes, to screw things up, destroy relationships and make everyone hate them.

When the proverbial hits the fan, when someone's wheels look like falling off or when they just need help, genuinely need help, to avoid a career crisis, you can bet your bottom dollar that if you haven't built trust with the recipient of your well-meaning feedback, then you've only got yourself to blame when their amygdalae kick in and they become defensive or emotional when you call them aside for a deep and meaningful.

Another thing that comes up often on employee surveys is poor performers not being managed and that there's a lack of feedback. Think they might be linked?

You see, humans actually need and want feedback. Just not in the way many people seem to experience or deliver it at work, either pussy-footing around, like my well-meaning boss's boss, or, the other favoured alternative, the verbal ambush. Neither works. At all.

Given so many people struggle on both ends of the amygdalae-driven mess that is so often a feedback discussion, here's an idea that I've found works. You can do it if you're new to the job, or been there a while. As Nike says, *just do it* if you want your life to be easier, especially for when you have to have challenging conversations.

This is one of those earn the right things and goes something like this: dring a 'benign' moment or team meeting, simply say to each team member individually or to the team as whole,

"Would it be okay if I ask you to let me know if I say, or do anything that could positively or negatively affect my career? And if you do I promise I'll say thank you? Great."Would it be okay if I do that with you too, and you'll say thank you too? Great. Just so we're clear, that goes for great stuff and the not so great okay? And how it will sound is something like, "Hey Jack, this is one of those times when I want to give you a heads up about something amazing/confusing you said in the meeting today".

What this means is, keeping up your 3:1 ratio of positives to negatives, that when the time comes when you need to make a 'withdrawal', such as giving some harder-to-hear feedback, then the 'withdrawal' doesn't take your relationship into the red.

Five Steps to Getting Things Back on Track

A word of warning, and I can't say this strongly enough: expect this to go pear-shaped, with amygdalae flying off all over the place if you haven't put in any spade work on earning the right, you haven't built trust or done any work on getting to know the real person sitting in front of you. You've been warned …

1. PREPARE

Not a blow-by-blow 'canned' script – you need to come across as sincere and natural – but think about what your intentions and goals are prior to delivering your feedback. Think about how you'll open the meeting, given that it's possible that the bouncers will be on full alert, on both sides.

2. SET THE TONE

I'm assuming you want to maintain a respectful, trusting relationship with this person. Hold the meeting in an appropriate and private space, and consider the timing. Both can impact the other person's readiness to listen.

3. DESCRIBE SPECIFIC BEHAVIOUR

Not global all-encompassing traits. If you hear yourself saying, 'you're too … ' STOP. Focus on the behaviour and support the person. People aren't their behaviours, and strengths can often be a double-edged sword.

4. THEIR VERSION OF EVENTS

People need the chance to respond, to give their side of the story, possibly additional information, a context or a reason, or their perspective. Listen. That's all. Demonstrate that you want to understand their point of view, not that you've already made up your mind.

5. COLLABORATE ON A SOLUTION

Work together to come up with a suitable solution for a way forward. Asking questions rather than giving answers can often lead to the person coming to the same conclusion or answer that you would want. Recall all that stuff about mindset – this is far more powerful, more likely to have impact and so be implemented, over you just telling them.

Happily of course, when you start to put in place some of the ideas in *Culture101* (even if it's by 'stealth' to start), over time you should find yourself having a lot less of these sorts of chats with your peeps.

LEAVE A LEGACY

- LEAD HAPPY, HEALTHY PEOPLE ... YOU'LL LEAVE BEHIND A HAPPY, HEALTHY COMPANY

- FROM SPARK TO SHINE – TOOLS AND RESOURCES FOR A THRIVING CULTURE

Chapter 11

LEAD HAPPY, HEALTHY PEOPLE ... YOU'LL LEAVE BEHIND A HAPPY, HEALTHY COMPANY

Great spirits have always encountered violent opposition from mediocre minds. The mediocre mind is incapable of understanding the man who refuses to bow blindly to conventional prejudices, and chooses instead to express his opinions courageously and honestly.

Albert Einstein

Every year, something like 20,000 to 30,000 new books on leadership are published, yet during the same period it seems like there's little if any discernible impact on those gob-smacking engagement scores. The lure of quant over qual, technical over adaptive, command and control, business-as-usual is apparently still quite strong.

Given all the very convincing stats the scientists and researchers have kindly provided for us, you've got to wonder (well I sure do) why people aren't scorching burn marks into the heavy-duty-commercial-use carpet as they line up to talk turkey to the powers that be about some long overdue changes.

But hey, as I've said a couple of times, I'm a realist and I know that some people, despite all the science in the world, will still see this as a being a bit out there, far-fetched, touchy-feely shit. This is despite the fact that what they're doing is clearly not working well at all, as they apparently get told year in, year out in their engagement surveys.

Culture 101, based on a strengths-based philosophy and positive leadership, is *not* about walking around with a Duchenne smile all day, only saying nice things, hugging people, and making sure everyone gets a 'prize'. As an old boss once said to me, 'There's nothing so unequal as treating unequal people equally'. Yeah, took me a while to get my head around it too, but then I got it. It's about credit and recognition where it's due, constructive feedback when it's necessary and learning both from what went wrong as well as what's worked and is still working – and that's individually as well as within the company.

It's about being a realistic optimist like Sir Earnest Shackleton; making deposits in each other's emotional bank accounts; about creating a place at work where there are enough positive moments, more than three positives to each negative, to get the best out of people's happy chemicals and hormones – serotonin, oxytocin, endorphins and dopamine.

Getting the best out of people, rather than milking them dry to get the most, means increased wellbeing, greater resilience and more creative ideas, for starters. All of which leads, of course, to leaving a legacy of improved productivity, happier clients, and ultimately more profit.

As I've said, no one needs to know you're embarking on your own personal campaign to turn your culture around to one that's more conducive to human thriving … oh, and a more profitable company … and happier clients …

When you start implementing some of the ideas in *Culture 101*, starting with yourself first, you'll begin to notice a shift in the way people react to you. It may be subtle at first, but enough for your reward centre to get addicted to the responses you get and the accompanying dopamine hits for you to want to keep at it. People like being around positive, realistic optimists, people who aren't red socks or energy vampires, but act like more of a mental vaccination, building up people's resilience, positive emotions, energy reserves and wellbeing.

As Barbara Fredrickson[50] found: 'Resilience is an inner resource that grows over time. Positive emotions fertilize this growth … can loosen negativity's grip … and put the brakes on depression's downward spiral' (and it's much cheaper and better for you than anti-depressants).

What's some of the specific benefits of a leader leaving a positive emotional wake?

- Those who positively energise others are higher performers. Position in the so-called 'energy network' is four times the predictor of performance compared to position in the information or influence network

- Positive energisers tend to enhance the work of others. People who interact with or are connected to energisers also perform better

- High performing firms had three times as many positive energising networks than low performing firms[51]

---

50 - *Positivity; Ground Breaking Research to Release Your Inner Optimist and Thrive,* Barbara Fredrickson, Oneworld, 2009

51 - *What Creates Energy in Organizations?* Baker, W., Cross, R., & Parker, A., Sloan

While I've been writing *Culture 101*, I've been thrilled to hear of several companies who are well ahead of the curve, have seen the light and have already got the nod from the exec team to start a full-scale roll out of the kind of things I've been talking about. One of them is my health insurance fund. Given health insurance companies fork out so much for 'cures', is it any wonder that they've got on to some science-backed prevention for their own peeps?

Some companies, intuitively maybe, have already been doing *Culture 101* stuff for years, some of them way before all the volume of research, science and stats became so widely available.

Unless your company is up for a boots-and-all, let's-do-it, *Culture 101* makeover, or you've got the enthusiastic ears of friends in high places at work, the way to go about implementing the ideas in *Culture 101* is little by little, starting with you. (If you need something to take to the unbelievers, the research-based list in the appendix might be a source of inspiration).

Start with some simple things like putting your listening skills on steroids if you need to, checking in with your mindset, outing any limiting beliefs and getting clear on your own core purpose and values.

Check your language, inside and outside of your head, and start 'watching your mouth'.

Find your favourite comedians to turn to when you're on a stress-fueled cortisol and adrenaline overload, tipping the balance back with a few dopamine, endorphin and serotonin hits (trust me, a few good solid LOL's – possibly somewhere private if you're at work – really works wonders to shift a negative mood).

If you start working, step-by-step, on implementing one idea at a time from *Culture 101*, you'll be well on your way to leaving a legacy when you move on. The Four Keys to a thriving culture are a great place to start, because, simply put, if you:

- **EARN THE RIGHT** – people will remember you because you really listened to them, you took them seriously; you helped them discover their own personal anchor to help through the difficult times; you were humble; you took the time to build trust with each of them and you shared some of your own stories to show who you are, and what to do when things aren't clear cut

- **ACHIEVE** – people will remember you because you helped them set realistic goals, helped them see how what they do each day for the company connects to their dreams; you showed the team how to win; you pitched in and helped when needed, always leaving your ego in the car park. And you had some fun doing it

- **COACH AND MENTOR** – people will remember you because you helped them to discover their strengths and showed them how to manage the not so fun tasks; because you were instrumental in getting rid of the annual performance review in favour of regular check in 'pre-view' chats; you helped redirect a fixed mindset; and because they could trust you to recognise and encourage them, and to not shy away from the tougher talk if needed

As you can see, you don't need anything much at all to start building a platform to leave a lasting positive legacy – just some determination, perseverance, stamina, faith in yourself and maybe, just maybe, by giving a nod and a wink to the underground *Culture 101* rebel in you.

Leadership is all about making others better as
a result of your presence, and making sure that
impact lasts in your absence.
Sheryl Sandberg

Appendix

FROM SPARK TO SHINE

TOOLS AND RESOURCES FOR A THRIVING CULTURE

I n the late 1990s, at the time when I was working with the 'flat liner' boss, I read the following story in the local paper. Reflecting on my own crying-on-the-way-to-work job, I fell about laughing as the implications of the poor dung beetles' plight struck me. Sharing the story with a fellow sufferer at work, we coined the term 'dung beetle syndrome' – Amanda and I still use the term to this day …

Concerned about the legendary and ever-growing blowfly problem in Australia, scientists struck on the great idea of importing dung beetles to deal with the excessive dung problem – which of course was attracting the flies. Areas were mapped out, beetles tagged and released and left to do their thing.

Now, I don't know how much you know about dung beetles, but they are mighty little creatures capable of disposing of huge amounts of dung many times their body weight, including most notably elephant dung. Pretty impressive.

157

After three months in the Aussie bush, the scientists went to see how the beetles were doing. Much to their surprise and dismay, the dung beetles hadn't made much of an impact on the situation. When the beetles were captured and assessed, the scientists described them as showing all the signs of extreme stress. There was, it seems, just too much shit – and so, dung beetle syndrome was born.

If dung beetle syndrome has hit you hard, the following is a list to have a browse through, perhaps along with checking out some of the books and articles I've mentioned, getting you started on your *Culture 101* journey, out of the mire, back on track and thriving once more.

Remember: any culture change happens one step at a time, starting with you.

RESOURCE	WHAT IS IT?	WHERE DO I FIND IT?
Positivity self-test	The positivity ratio from Barbara Fredrickson takes about one minute to complete and gives you a snapshot of your Positive to Negative ratio for a 24-hour period.	www.positivityratio.com
Learned Optimism Test	Adapted from Dr. Martin Seligman's book *Learned Optimism*, this quick quiz gives you a snapshot of how optimistic you are right now.	http://web.stanford.edu

Strengths Spotting	*The Top Ten Strengthspotting Tips* from Alex Linley in PDF format.	https://strath.ac.uk www.capp.co
Values in Action	Discover your character strengths and the core values that drive your behaviour with this free 10-minute on-line survey.	www.viacharacter.org
Play at Work	There are many websites with a wide range of ideas on how to institute some lightheartedness at work. Not all will appeal or be relevant; some may be a bit too 'out there' for you. Just surf around the net and find what's most likely to work for you and your team.	www.daringtolivefully.com www.snacknation.com www.10000stepsaustralia.com
Recognition	Some comprehensive lists of no and low cost ideas on how to recognise employees. Again, not all will work for you, but I'm sure you'll find a couple of ideas you can use.	https://www.americanexpress.com/articles 101 Ways to Reward Employees (Without Giving Them Cash) www.forbes.com/sites 25 Low Cost Ways to Reward Employees https://www/fastcompany.com/articles Low-Cost Ways to Show Employees They're Highly Valued

Laughter	Some professional laughter resource sites. Also, if you're up for it, check out the local laughter yoga groups near you.	www.laughteronlineuniversity.com www.holisticservices.com.au www.laughterforliving.com.au
Good News Websites	A change from all the bad news we're flooded with, these websites provide some balance, highlighting some of the good stuff that's happening out there.	www.dailygood.com www.brainpickings.org www.goodnewsnetwork.com
How we Feel	A daily or hourly check-in app that helps build self-awareness and Emotional Intelligence	https://howwefeel.org
Mindfulness	There's a load of websites and apps, many free, to help with all sorts of applications for mindfulness. From mindful eating to playing and maintaining focus on tasks through to being creative.	www.mindful.org http://pocketmindfulness.com Insight app for Android
Mindset	This free mindset quiz helps to show where you may have a fixed rather than a growth mindset. Fixed mindsets tend to get in the way of achieving goals in certain areas of our lives.	www.edpartnerships.org

About the Author

PENNY NESBITT

After years of studying, reading and standing on her feet talking about all things culture and leadership, no one was more surprised than Penny to find herself seated for extended periods of time, writing her first book.

But as one client said with the utmost of admiration, after twenty years of 'banging on about it', a book seemed like the way to go.

Hailing originally from Melbourne (still secretly loves it), then spending her teen years in Canberra, Penny spent half a lifetime in beautiful Sydney before moving back to the capital of cool before word got out. Canberra, yes Canberra.

In between learning and development gigs, she has a love-hate relationship with a Reformer (of the Pilates kind), is a closet knitter (yoga for the brain) and, as far as she knows, hasn't poisoned anyone yet at one of her legendary dinner parties.

Penny's also now sought after as a guest speaker, coach and facilitator of all things *Culture 101*, and in between is a convert to Netflix, her drug of choice for boxed-set sustenance being Earl Grey tea, a couch buddy and her two dogs.

She fesses up to a further addiction to learning, inhales books, is a would-be neuroscientist and a devotee of all things Positive Psychology.

You can contact her at:

penny@pennynesbitt.com.au